WHAT IS A
Selfish Baby Mama?

BY: ABLYSS GILLESPIE & ONNEY

PUBLISHED BY:
ONNEY PUBLISHING & PERFORMANCES, INC.

A Word from Our Authors

Alyss

When I gave birth to my little girl, I was more scared of childbirth than what was to come after I held her in my arms for the first time. While creating "What is a Selfish Baby Mama", I had to take a good look in the mirror. In the beginning, some fathers are truly scared when they find out a woman is having their baby, let alone a child from a woman they have no intention on being with.

Hopefully, having a child is exciting for both parents, but the biggest fear of many fathers, especially the non-custodial fathers, is not having hands-on daily support and decision making for the best interest of the child. Listening to the fathers was emotional, but catching an earful from the children brought tears to my eyes.

When I spoke with other baby mamas in reference to their behavior and how they handled certain situations, I was excited to put pen to pad and get to work on exposing how some baby mamas are truly selfish and overly controlling. When I look back on some discussions held with my child's father, I can admit I was controlling the situation and not allowing him to assist in decision making. Many of the baby daddies interviewed really poured their hearts out; they were filled with anger, confusion, heartache and disbelief.

The biggest hang-up is trust. A few of the fathers interviewed feel their baby mamas are equivalent to a stranger on the street; they just do not know or understand them. Since I am not a father, it is truly hard for me to understand from their perspective and viewpoint. While listening, some of their stories I truly could relate to, like hanging up the phone in my baby daddy's face, taking my octave higher than normal, and really taking the face-to-face communication to a stressful level.

There are plenty of fathers in the world raising their children alone, but then there are fathers limited to following the paperwork provided by the Attorney General's office. Finally, there are some fathers not allowed to see their kids at all. When speaking to some fathers, it was hard to hear how many of the baby mamas would refuse visitation if child support wasn't paid. The big one was not answering the door for every other weekend's visitation. My face was in total shock. As I strolled through social media, I saw many fathers begging and hoping their baby mamas would lighten up. It really hit home and inspired me to assist these fathers in getting their stories heard.

Having the courage to write a book expressing the selfish side of baby mamas really spoke to my conscience and spirit. My relationship with my own father is phenomenal. I saw him every day growing up as a child, and all the precious moments we spent together will never leave me. I encourage all fathers to keep fighting and not give up; your children need you.

-Ablyss

Olney

It took great courage to begin on this journey of reflection and testimony. Although I'd like to think that I would be the model "Baby Mama", listening to others share their stories made me re-evaluate the scale on which I'd weighed myself. The transparency revealed that I, too, had been selfish at times.

Looking back on my childhood, there were times when my father was unable to provide financially towards my care, and I'd always believed that it was due to his inability to provide that he was unable to see me. I was wrong in that matter, but needless to say, there are many mothers that share that exact sentiment. They feel that if the father is unable to provide financial assistance, his role in the child's life should be as void as the financial help. Therefore, his role is extremely marginalized in the child's life.

In hindsight, I realized that throughout my adolescent years, I blamed my mother for the absence of my father. Eventually the cycle continued.

Although I pride myself on the fact that I never prevented my sons from spending time with their father, I didn't always do my part to keep the co-parenting relationship magnanimous. I was financially secure, therefore, I neglected the need for their father to be in their lives. Somehow, the cycle, no matter how right or wrong, had unintentionally continued through me.

I have always believed that the first step to corrective behavior is to acknowledge the areas where corrections or reinforcements are needed. Although many of the mothers that can be found in these selfish categories will have the courage to admit their selfish behavior, the true test begins when she exhibits the fortitude to improve, and tenacity to do her part in the betterment of the co-parenting relationship.

Could you be one of the parents that are found within these pages? Or are you on the other end of the scale? Take a read and see...

-Onney

Preface

$\mathcal{T}$he feelings and emotions of not being able to add in the decision-making process and assist in handling in-home decisions is hard on the non-custodial parent; simultaneously, it can consciously or unconsciously create hardships on the custodial parent when doing it all by oneself or not allowing the non-custodial parent to assist. This book explains what the other parent is thinking, even if the comments or expressions may come across as adverse, unfavorable, or contravening. It is in the best interest of the child/children for both parents to maintain healthy communication; if this can't happen, then it is important to seek proper assistance.

Single mothers and fathers are everywhere, and in some cases, both parents truly want what is best for the child or children. Have the following questions and/or statements ever come to mind?

- Why would he/she say this about me? I am a great parent.
- Why would you not want me to spend more time with our child?
- Why does he/she say the meanest things to me?
- What did I do to deserve all of this havoc? I want what is best and I can make sure of this better than he/she.

The above questions can come across as selfish to some, if answered a certain way. One parent can appear selfish based on his or her past experiences with another parent, family, or just life in general. Which one are you?

- Do I respond the way I do as a defense mechanism?
- Do I handle situations the way I do to hurt the other parent's feelings out of resentment?
- Is it my way or the highway?

Do you really know if you fit the category of being self-indulgent, self-interested, and self-seeking? Does the other parent get you to a point of having to place a guard up? Do you appear to come across as parsimonious, ungenerous, or vain? If you see yourself within these pages, are you able to find the most positive way to correct yourself? If you see yourself within these pages, how can you handle the situation differently?

Some may find this book offensive, some may find it refining and refreshing, while others may just find it practical and helpful. In the end, the child is the most important factor within the equation.

It's on you to figure out if you are, or want to be, the opposite of what's read within these pages. It's up to you as the reader to figure out if benevolence, kindheartedness, or being magnanimous are character traits which you would like to possess, not for the benefit of the other parent, but in the best interest of the child. Some of the expressions in this book may guide parents into being better co-parents. We, as authors, are hoping both parents can and will improve at co-parenting.

"What is a Selfish Baby Mama?" is geared towards raising awareness on social parenting issues that arise involving mothers whether single, divorced, or married, whether they are raising the children alone or living with the fathers but still feel as if they are doing the job alone. This book will highlight some of the scenarios that cause dysfunctionality in a single and co-parenting environment. We would like to thank all the "Baby Mamas and Baby Daddies" who assisted us in bringing subjects to light and for allowing us to use your stories to ensure the success of this book.

ABOUT THE AUTHORS

ABLYSS

$\mathcal{M}$elanie Wilson, also known as Ablyss Gillespie, was born and raised in Missouri City, Texas, and graduated from Willowridge High School in 1995.

After moving back to Houston from Memphis, Tennessee, life's events encouraged her to express herself through art and music. In 2003, she joined the Houston poetry scene where she met various other artists, collaborated with them, and became truly inspired. This is how she met Lanora Laws, known to the world as Onney.

Ironically, Abylss was raised one street over from Onney, and they both attended the same high school. Ablyss actually graduated with Onney's brother. On the poetry scene, Ablyss tapped into her skills of playwright. She presented her first play at Catfish Willy's, entitled, "Acceptance Shadow" in front of an audience of dozens over a weekend. Expanding from this excitement, Ablyss decided to continue developing productions. Her second production, "Intimidation vs. Intimidation", was showcased at local restaurants and rental facilities.

Eventually, she decided she wanted to move her productions to black box theaters. While "Intimidation vs. Intimidation" was showing at the legendary Silver House Theater, Ablyss began working with Jonathan Dale Samuels, whom she had met some years before. The CEO of *Dahrk* Sity Productions, Jonathan, a.k.a Kik-A-Flo, partnered with Abylss to work on music. Some of his ideas and inspirational styles helped to mold and create a certain essence, which she added to her future productions. Currently, Abylss uses his style of music and creative beats in all of her stage plays.

After the run of her first play at The Silver House Theatre, she penned another play entitled, "Submission Adultery Disease", and while writing this production, Ablyss hit Kosmic Oasis, a known studio for underground artists owned by K'monte, to record "Mama's Titty", her jazz single. Ablyss desired to do everything on a bigger scale so she held a concert event entitled, "Dusty Records" and there, she let the world in on her singing abilities and surprised everyone with her poetry book entitled "Cycle of Alteration", published by Onney Publishing & Performances, Inc.

Following this success, Ablyss went on to showcase "Submission Adultery Disease" (S.A.D.) at The Silver House Theater. Shortly afterward, Ablyss became pregnant with her daughter, who is autistic. Being a mother takes up most of her time, but she has traveled to New York on several occasions to perform on the legendary SOB stage with Kindred Family and was the opening act for Eric Roberson.

The behavior of Ablyss's daughter became a bit much for her caregivers to handle, so she took a short break from music, theater, and writing to focus on her little one. After getting her daughter where she needed her to be, Ablyss was hired for a Walmart commercial and an Aspire Network commercial.

She also directed the stage play entitled, "Badu-Izms: A Tribute to Erykah Badu", and showcased "*Bougie*, Broke, and Single", (formerly known as "Intimidation vs. Intimidation") a year later.

During this time, Ablyss also graduated college, receiving her Bachelor's and Master's Degree in Leadership, while minoring in Non-profit Management from Northeastern University online in Boston, Massachusetts. To assist her in understanding the non-profit sector, Ablyss was the President for two years over the Willowridge Mighty Eagle Band Booster Club. While leading the club, she put together various fundraiser talent shows to assist in raising money. Volunteering her time for the booster club was one of the best times of her life. As CEO of Zalyn's Inc.; a company that specializes in event coordinating, Ablyss is happy to continue her love for art, writing, and productions.

ONNEY

*W*hile the males of the industry continue to dominate, a lesser gratitude is paid to their female counterparts. Along comes Onney, to counter the perception with her no-nonsense demeanor mixed with a spirited personality. As a member of the celebrated Laws family (Ronnie, Hubert, Eloise and Debra), Onney has created a strong following in her career as well.

Onney is a writer and poet who addresses a wide range of life's issues. She is an insightful hip-hop poetess who uses her incendiary vocal skills to take us into the erotica of love and the morass of social and political issues that concern us all. Her observations are laced with wisdom beyond her years and sautéed in humor that holds the listener or the reader rapt.

Although Onney's first love has always been poetry, the Houston-bred poet has experienced unbridled success not only on-stage, but off-stage as an author. She is also CEO of her publishing company, "Onney Publishing & Performances, Inc.", which has become a lauded template and formula for upstart and thriving authors looking for success. Onney published her first book "Infinite Silhouettes" in 2007. She then went on to publish "Cycle of Alteration" by Ablyss Gillespie, "Old Skool's Sex Tools" (Volumes I, II & III) by Howard McAfee, "In Its Entirety" by Aja Fitzgerald, and "Praying for a Better Day" by Marquis Jonkins to name a few. Onney perfected her craft in journalism and editing as the Entertainment Editor and columnist for the

"Houston Sun Newspaper" from the years of 2008-2011.

The talented thespian is equally praised for her work on the screen and stage as an actor, songwriter, singer and model. Onney has performed at venues across the country, opening for Ron Isley, Angela Winbush, BET Comedians Shawn Harris, Shang & Michael Blackston, along with actor and author Darrin Henson, and many more. She is featured on Houston rapper & radio personality Kiotti's CD, entitled "Almost Famous", as well as Houston rapper Mankyne's mix tape released in 2014, entitled "Serve-All Mix Tape".

As a feature artist and actress, Onney appears in 'Rent-A-Car', executively produced by Frank White, where she performs her hit single, "*October*". She also featured in "A Gangland's Love Story", executively produced by Greg Carter, where she performs "*Mr. Incredible*". She received writer's credit in "A Gangland's Love Story" for writing the poems recited in the movie by Reagan Gomez, A.J. Lamas and herself. Two songs from her album, "BeYou2Feel Music" were also selected for the movie's soundtrack. Both films were picked up by Maverick (owned by Madonna) and can be found in your local Redbox.

Onney landed her first major role in a stage play when she auditioned for Submission Adultery Disease (S.A.D.), a play written and directed by Ablyss Gillespie. This play was held in the historical Silver House Theatre located in Houston, Texas. Acting opened Onney up to a whole new avenue of expression. She has also shared the stage with The Legendary Shirley Murdock while maintaining the lead female role in the gospel stage play tour

"Heaven Ain't Hard to Find," directed by Curtis Von, the lead male role, and produced by 3Wise Men Productions.

After taking a brief hiatus, in 2012, Onney performed at the Def Poetry Jam Summit put on by Co-Founder Danny Simmons in front of a crowd of 5,000+ at the Miller Outdoor Theatre in Houston, Texas. She was then cast for the stage play and movie "Lyfe's Poetic Revenge", a play written and directed by Rae-Shell D. Fletcher, where she played the double role of Bridgett and also herself. The play was held at the Country Playhouse Theatre in Houston. Soon thereafter, Onney landed another major role in a stage play when she featured in "*Bougie,* Broke & Single" a play written and directed by Ablyss Gillespie and held at the Hobby Center in Houston.

In 2013, Onney received the "Woman of the Year Award" presented by the Houston Sun Newspaper and the City of Houston. The guest speakers on her behalf consisted of Congresswoman Sheila Jackson Lee, Mayor Annise Parker, Congressman Al Green and many more. She was honored for her community participation in Adopt-A-Diva Camps, a program that mentors young girls from the ages of 12-18, as well as her contributions annually in Juneteenth Celebrations at the historical Emancipation Park located in 3rd Ward Houston.

Although Onney's resume seems substantial, her accomplishments did not come easily. Coming from a lineage of talent was great, but Onney chose not to use her roots as a pass to open doors, thus changing her name from Lanora Laws to Onney (Meaning: *To desire to be great*). Onney (Lanora Laws-Jackson) was born and raised in Houston, Texas. Onney became a mother to her first son at the young age of 16. Even with the challenge of being a teen mother, Onney graduated from Willowridge High School at 16 and went on to become MS Certified and receive her Bachelor's in Business Administration with a Minor in Accounting from the University of Honolulu on a scholarship.

Onney is the proud mother of 3 sons, now ages 20, 17, and 12; the majority of their years were spent being raised by her alone. Onney has overcome many trials and set-backs in her life from becoming a teen mother, to experiencing divorce, and even becoming temporarily paralyzed, but she refused to let anything sway her from her goals.

Most recently, Onney and Ablyss decided to create Selfish Subjects Inc., a joint venture in which they bring their creative talents together to educate the world on social issues as well as provide entertainment. Coincidentally, Onney & Ablyss attended the same high school and lived one block away from one another while growing up. Yet they did not cross paths until they joined the creative world of the poetry scene in Houston. After working together on multiple projects, these ladies couldn't deny the creative chemistry and desire they both shared for the arts. It only made sense to join forces in creating great reads for years to come.

Onney recently remarried and resides in Missouri City, Texas, with her husband and children. With both she and her husband having children from previous marriages, creating a blended family has helped her to gain a whole new understanding on how co-parenting from different households can be an extensive challenge to all involved. Who better to author a book of this nature than someone that has experience from every angle?

TABLE OF CONTENTS

self·ish
selfiSH/
adjective
adjective: **selfish**

1. (of a person, action, or motive) lacking consideration for others; concerned chiefly with one's own personal profit or pleasure.

"I joined them for selfish reasons"

synonyms:
egocentric, egotistic, egotistical, egomaniacal, self-centered, self-absorbed, self-obsessed, self-seeking, self-serving, wrapped up in oneself;
inconsiderate, thoughtless, unthinking, uncaring, uncharitable;
mean, miserly, grasping, greedy, mercenary, acquisitive, opportunistic;
informal looking after number one
"he is just selfish by nature"

antonyms: altruistic

1: concerned excessively or exclusively with oneself: seeking or concentrating on one's own advantage, pleasure, or well-being without regard for others

2: arising from concern with one's own welfare or advantage in disregard of others <a *selfish* act>

1

***

I
Don't care
If the child *is* with
You all the time,
You still gone pay
Child support!!

***

Her Bills His Money

Marquise and Tish had been divorced for 10 years, and since the divorce, Marquise never missed a child support payment. Up until recently, Tish had been doing quite well for herself. But about eight months ago, Tish lost her job and had not been able to find stable employment.

Although Tish was receiving child support, it was not enough to maintain all the bills that she would incur on a monthly basis. Marquise had no problem helping when he could, but with the $625 that he was already sending to Tish, his income was pretty fixed.

Marquise suggested that Tish allow their son to live with him. Besides, he was almost 13 years old. Although Marquise felt that Tish had done a great job, it was time for him to teach his son important things about becoming a man.

For three months, Marquise had been raising their son alone, with Tish only getting him on the weekends. Both Tish and Marquise had agreed that she would reimburse any child support payments that she received while her son was with him, but Tish did not keep her word. Marquise had to go back and forth to the child support office to get it corrected.

The Attorney General's office advised him that he would need to get a lawyer and file for custody before they would stop garnishing his checks for child support.

Not only does Marquise have to take care of his son without any financial assistance from Tish, but $625 is still coming out of his paycheck.

How Selfish

Lies for No Reason

BD: I will come and pick you up around 5:00p.m.

Child: Okay Daddy, see you then.

(Momma calls baby daddy and asks to change the time to a few hours later because she's doing something with the child.)

BM: I don't think he is coming. It's now 6:00p.m., and he should have been here an hour ago. Let's go get some ice cream and go to the mall since he didn't show up.

Child: Can I just wait for him?

BM: Wait for him? Why would you do that? Your daddy should come when he says he is going to come.

(Mother arrives home with the child, and the child immediately goes to bed. The phone rings.)

BM: Hello.

BD: I came by at 7:00p.m. to pick up our child like you said, and no one was there. What's up with that?

BM: Something came up.

BD: You said something came up at 5:00p.m. and asked me to change to 7:00p.m. Then I call your cell phone, and you didn't answer.

BM: Look something came up so make plans some

other time. *(hangs up phone)*

Next Time, Don't Be Late

BD: I am going to be about 30 minutes late picking up Samiya.

BM: Well I have something to do, so I guess this weekend should just pass, and maybe you can be on time to get her the next assigned weekend.

BD: Can you please just work with me? I had a client that extended longer than I thought it would.

BM: Again, I have something to do, and we are not going to be here. Bye.

Oh Well

$\mathcal{S}$tacy had been in an on-again, off-again relationship with her ex-fiancé Jeff for over 5 years. Prior to their final breakup, they experienced one of their off-again moments, and Stacy began dating Robert, a guy she met through a friend. It wasn't long after dating her new interest that she and Jeff decided that they would give their love one last try. Stacy immediately ended the relationship with Robert to work on things with Jeff.

Jeff loved Stacy with all of his heart, and although they had a turbulent relationship at times, Jeff knew that Stacy was the woman he wanted to marry. After several months of working towards getting back to their happy place in the relationship, Jeff asked Stacy to marry him. Stacy gladly accepted.

Two weeks after making the engagement announcement, a complicated twist was added to their relationship when Stacy discovered that she was pregnant. The pregnancy would have been great news to Stacy, if only Jeff was the father! Based on the calculations and her projected due date, she knew that there was no way that this child was Jeff's. She tried to think of several different scenarios that would help Jeff understand, but she couldn't think of any. Instead, she never said a word to Jeff that the child she carried belonged to Robert.

Jeff had his own reservations about the pregnancy and the timing, but felt that there was no way that Stacy would keep something like that from

8

him. Not his Stacy. As Jeff allowed the idea of fatherhood to settle, he could hardly hide the excitement. Jeff's family knew how he felt about fatherhood and family. Before long, everyone shared the same sentiment, and the excitement became contagious. Throughout Stacy's pregnancy, she became irritable and downright rude to Jeff, which caused a strain on their already fragile relationship. However, being the man that Jeff was, it was easy to blame the mood swings on the hormonal changes caused by the pregnancy. When the time came for the delivery of the baby, Jeff was right there holding Stacy's hand. When it came time to sign the birth certificate, Jeff signed it with pride in his heart; all he ever wanted was a son to call his own.

After the birth of Jacari, their relationship took a turn for the worse, and Jeff decided that he would end things with Stacy and be a father to his son regardless of their relationship status. Several months after the breakup, Jeff was served with a court subpoena for a child support hearing. Truth be told, he always had an inkling that Jacari was not his son, but could not pull himself to mention it to Stacy, as he knew that would indeed insult her. As a result, his uncertainty was left unanswered.

Their day in court...

Judge: I hereby order you to pay $750.00 a month in child support and ensure that medical insurance is provided for the child.

Jeff couldn't believe that Stacy had done this to him. He couldn't seem to understand why she needed to get the courts involved when he had went above and beyond to care for Jacari. Nevertheless, he paid and provided as ordered.

Several weeks after court, Stacy went to visit her sister Erin, and the discussion came up about what had transpired in court earlier that month. Stacy's sister, Erin, was the only person that knew that Jacari was really Robert's son. Stacy went on to explain that Jeff was ordered to pay $750.00. Erin looked at Stacy with a confused look and asked her, "Girl, how can you sleep at night knowing darn well that isn't that man's kid?"

Stacy looked her dead in the eye and replied, "I know the baby is not his, but hey, he signed the birth certificate, so oh well!!!"

How Selfish...

*
***

If he wanted the baby to have his last name, he should have married me.

***
*

Your Daddy Don't Want You

$\mathcal{T}$abitha was a young and beautiful actress that seemed to have everything going for her. She had achieved her master's degree, opened her own law firm and somehow had time to master her acting career. She had done all of this while maintaining the role of a single mother. Her son Bryson was 9 years old and it seemed that he was beginning to ask about his father's whereabouts more often.

When Bryson was a little younger, he'd only ask about his father during holidays like Father's Day, Christmas, or his birthday, but he began asking about his father as frequently as twice a month. Tabitha had made several attempts to reach Tyson, Bryson's father. But every attempt ended in an argument with disrespectful connotations. Tabitha was still holding onto resentment for the way Tyson had treated her and denied that Bryson was his. Tyson's argument was that he knew that she had dated someone else during the time that their encounter took place, so how could he be blamed? Nevertheless, it left a sour taste in Tabitha's mouth for him. She resented the public embarrassment of having to prove that she knew who her son's father was.

The constant arguments made the co-parenting environment so unbalanced, that the only time Tabitha and Tyson reached a solution, was in the courtroom. Although Tyson had weekend visitation rights, Tabitha wouldn't let Tyson come to see Bryson until he'd make some effort to pay his child support. Tabitha also resented that Tyson hadn't made a child support payment in two years.

As Tabitha was losing patience trying to communicate with Tyson, she decided that she didn't need him around, and neither did her son. Contrary to her belief, Bryson needed just that: his father.

Several months had gone by, and Tabitha started dating a fellow cast mate that she had known for years. She was happier than she had ever been and became heavily distracted by her new love interest. She decided that it was time to introduce her son to her good friend, now beaux, Steven.

Meeting Steven caused a new curiosity in Bryson, which caused him to ask about his father's whereabouts whenever Steven was around. This would always cause an awkward silence in the room. Steven had known Tabitha for several years, but this was something he knew nothing about. Tabitha had never allowed him to meet her son, so he had never really questioned her about her son's father's whereabouts either. His only concern was that she was single, and he wasn't imposing on another man's territory. No harm, no foul, right?

Tyson had made several attempts to reach Tabitha since their last court date. However, that was four months ago. Her number remained the same, but her address had changed, and he had already been court ordered to stay away from her place of practice. He wasn't in a position to make a financial contribution due to a chain of events that had landed him in the unemployment line. It seemed that once he totaled his car after losing his job, he hadn't been able to recover, physically or financially. He would take whatever jobs he could get, but without a dependable car and income, he was back at home with his mother and father until he could get back on his feet. Although Tyson was not making any financial contributions, he wanted to be a part of his son's life, and his son wanted him there.

Tabitha had struggled since Bryson was born. She had achieved many of her goals, but the sacrifices she made to raise Bryson alone while attempting to reach her goals, had caused her to resent the freedom that Tyson was able to flaunt around by not being accountable.

It was Bryson's first football game of the season, and Tabitha and Steve had big plans for Bryson after the game. Bryson asked Tabitha to call his dad and ask him to attend the game. With all of the plans that she and Steven had made for Bryson, she didn't want him to be distracted with a once-in-a season popup from his father. Steven and Tabitha had been dating over a year and were living together.

Since Tabitha's decision to agree to her and Steven's living arrangements, Steven had been there to take Bryson to football practice, the barber shop, and simply stand in the gap as a male role model. Somehow, Tabitha believed that because Steven was there to fill the gap that he would suffice as a replacement.

Bryson had grown to really enjoy Steven's company, but he missed his dad. He sometimes wished that Steven really was Tyson. He wondered why his dad didn't ever come to any of his games. He wondered why he didn't call him on birthdays.

Tabitha knew. Tabitha had moved on with her life. She was happy, successful, and had found the man of her dreams. She didn't concern herself with matters that had anything to do with Tyson, despite him being the father of her son.

It was so peaceful in Tabitha's life. Her firm was doing great, Bryson seemed to be excelling in academics, and a happily ever after was definitely on the horizon. Those complicated conversations she once had with her son's father were a thing of the past.

The game was about to begin, and Bryson became antsy.

"Mom! Mom! Did you talk to my dad? Is he coming?" he asked in a tone filled with anxiousness.

Tabitha immediately looked at Steven to read his expression, but he stood there with a blank stare. Steven never really showed any reaction whenever the topic of Tyson was brought up.

Without much thought, Tabitha responded with dishonesty.

"I called him, but I was unable to reach him. I sent him a text message, but I wouldn't worry about it if I were you, son. Besides, Steven and I are here for you always."

Bryson ran off toward the field with hopes that his dad would arrive to see him play his new position as the quarterback. He had practiced all summer and wanted to show his dad how far he could throw. Unbeknown to Bryson, his father had never received that call.

After the game, Bryson remained gloomy through the remainder of the evening. His team had won, and his mom had planned a huge after-party for the entire team at the city's indoor arcade, theme park and race track, sponsored by her firm. Steven had bought him the hover board that he had been asking about since Christmas, but even with everything that was going on around Bryson, he felt empty inside. He was sad, so sad, that it was turning into resentment. He resented his dad for not being there, he resented Steven for not being Tyson, and he resented Tabitha for loving Steven more than she loved his dad. He started to wonder why his mom made his dad go away.

Tabitha, unaware to what was going on with her son emotionally, perceived it as another one of Bryson's 'spoiled child' episodes. She gave him the world. He was able to participate in everything he would ask for. Football, Band, AAU basketball, Tae Kwon Do, you name it... His clothing line consisted of everything brand name, and his mother lived in the best of neighborhoods. He had every game system an 11-year-old could ask for, and yet he was still walking around with his mouth stuck out.

While the group had rushed over to the line for the race cars, Tabitha noticed that Bryson had walked away from the group. Bryson was no longer participating with the group. Tabitha took this opportunity to pull Bryson to the side and set him straight. He was not going to embarrass her in front of all these parents and coaches. She tapped Steven on his shoulder to signal him to stay behind while pointing towards Bryson before walking his way.

"Bryson! Bryson! What is wrong with you! You can never be grateful! What's the problem this time?" she said with a fire in her eyes. She clinched her teeth with her hands on her hips.

"Why can't he ever be here?" Bryson looked up and asked with tears welled in his eyes.

Taken aback from the question, Tabitha blurted out, "Your daddy doesn't want you!!!"

At that very moment, Bryson and Tyson's relationship was broken without any effort from either of them. Tyson was calling Tabitha, but Tabitha was declining his calls. Bryson was constantly asking about his father's whereabouts, but his mother was not being honest about why his father was not showing up physically.

How Selfish...

Child Support.
Is my Money...
I can do
What the
Hell I
Want with
it!!!!

96 Hours, Nothing More...

She confines me to 96 hours a month only...
(with the exception of the 5th weekend)

There are so many more days in the week and other
weekends that I can spend time with our little one,
but she will not let me.

I have to follow the paperwork from the Attorney
General's office.

Instead of working with me, she would rather throw
it in my face that I chose not to be with her.

...and since I chose not to be with her, I am limited to
only the stamp mark of 96.

How Selfish...

SINCE YOU
CHOSE
TO MARRY
HER
THEN YOU
CAN KISS GOODBYE TO
EVER SEEING
YOUR CHILD AGAIN!

Premeditated Entrapment

*A*mber and Carl had been in an undefined love affair since their college years. At first, it was fun and exciting to be able to have the intimacy of a relationship without the restraints of the commitment that comes along with it.

Whenever they would get together, it was always a party. They were free spirits that lived life on the edge. Amber was in love with Carl, but she knew if she pressed the issue and asked him to go into details about how he felt about her, that he would be turned off, and she'd essentially push him away. This is not what Amber wanted. She wanted more than the late night rendezvous after sneaking out of the dorm, or the secret movie dates where they would meet in the back row to make out. She was growing tired of being a *Secret Lover*.

Whenever they were around their friends, Carl treated Amber like one of the fellas. There was nothing romantic about that. Soon her girlfriends started to believe that the secret love affair that she had told them about was all in her imagination, and Amber was telling them that just to take him off the market and away from them. Besides, Carl was the star quarterback and voted "Most Popular Gent of the Year". He was what the girls called 'Boyfriend Material': perfect smile, perfect skin, tall, dark, handsome, smart and mannerable.

He could practically have any girl he wanted back then, and not much had changed. It seemed that Amber had gotten accustomed to doing whatever she thought would make Carl happy. After they both graduated from college, they didn't see each other as much, but when they did get together, it was as if they had never been apart.

The meeting would always lead to intimacy in some form or fashion. Amber couldn't help but notice that Carl was no longer treating her like one of the fellas. He treated her like a woman, a grown woman! The naughty things that he would do to her made her feel alive.

One night, the two of them were walking into the parking garage after leaving a party at his frat brother's loft. As they reached the car, he made love to her right there on the hood where anyone walking by could see. She found that to be so exhilarating about him. So whatever his fantasies were, she tried to fulfill them, all of them.

Carl liked Amber and even loved her to an extent. He enjoyed what they shared, but he knew that she wasn't going to be "the one". She was fun. She was his party girl that would do whatever he wanted, and that was cool. But Carl yearned for something different. He wanted a good girl. A sophisticated lady, one whom attended the Mosque; one his mother would approve of. He just didn't see those qualities in Amber.

Amber wasn't like that with everyone, despite what Carl thought. Carl was the only man that ever had the ability to get her to do the things that she was willing to do to make him happy. Prior to meeting Carl, she never even thought about kissing a girl, but Carl had wanted to see her do it, so she did. Being that daredevil who Carl cheered on in the background actually ended up making her look weak-minded and gullible.

Doing whatever Carl asked her to do was something that Amber never seemed to outgrow. As a result, Carl still looked at her as the same easily influenced college girl that would do anything he dared her to do. That was not the "wifey type" that he had envisioned for his future.

Let it be noted that comfort breeds carelessness, and over the years, the two of them had become so comfortable with their intimate relationship that sometimes they would skip out on the prophylactics if Amber wasn't ovulating.

What Carl failed to mention to Amber was that he had been in a committed relationship for the last year and a half. What Amber failed to mention to Carl was that she knew he was in a relationship, but was waiting on him to say something. Since he didn't say anything, neither did she; instead, she went straight into planning mode.

She was not going to let somebody come and steal her man after she had been waiting on him for all of these years. She loved him, and she was not going to get kicked out of his life by anyone. She was going to make herself a permanent fixture in Carl's life, one way or another.

Amber had been off her birth control for well over six months. She was waiting for the perfect time to hook up with Carl. Amber wanted to be sure that she'd be ovulating. She had been taking supplements to assist in her ability to conceive in order to deter any problems that may have come from being on birth control for so long. She had it all figured out, and guess what? It worked!!!

Not only did it work, Amber waited until she was almost five months pregnant before telling Carl about the pregnancy. She wanted to make sure he couldn't force her to have an abortion, so she waited until after the sex of the baby could be determined by ultrasound.

As Carl began thinking about what he wanted out of his future, he realized that he had everything he needed in Lynne, his girlfriend of almost two years. She was smart, intelligent, independent, classy, spiritual, loving, lady-like and absolutely stunning. His on-going fling that he had with Amber was merely out of greed and convenience. He knew that he could get away with it, no strings attached, or so he thought... but he was ready to cut all ties with Amber in that way. He wanted to be faithful to the woman he considered asking to take his last name.

But it was too late. Amber was well over 4 months pregnant and one step closer to being a permanent fixture in his life. Carl had rarely made time to see Amber since his focus was elsewhere and that made it easier for her to hide the pregnancy from him. They lived 45 minutes away from one another, so it was easy for two or three weeks to pass without them seeing each other. But it had been two months, and so much had changed.

"Hey Amber. I'm on your side of town exiting the beltway, you home?" Carl asked into the receiver of his earpiece as he was closing the top on his convertible. He took the exit towards Amber's apartment.

"Yes, why? You coming to see me? You mean to tell me you care if I am still breathing over here?" Amber responded with sarcasm and slight laughter. "Yeah I'm home, how long it's going to be before you get here?" she continued.

"I'll be pulling up in about 10 minutes. I won't be able to stay long though, I just need to come speak with you about something and I don't want to do it over the phone," explained Carl.

"Ok, come on, I'm here," she responded as she wondered what could be so pressing. Needless to say, though, she needed to talk to him about a few things as well.

After hanging up the phone, she hurried to freshen up as she wanted to be presentable, and she grabbed her Chanel robe to cover her now-protruding belly. Before she sprung the news on him, she wanted to see what brought him out on her side of town first.

As Carl made his way into the apartment, he knew that ending this affair he had going on with Amber was something that he needed to do, no matter how difficult it would be. Regardless of what he may have thought of her in regards to the type of woman he preferred, she had been a true friend. He didn't want to hurt her, but seeing Lynne happy meant more.

"Amber, this isn't easy for me, but I need to be honest with you, and myself. I've been in a relationship for quite some time and I love her. I don't want to hurt her by cheating on her with you. We can still be friends, but I just want to be sure that

I put all my cards out on the table. I don't want to sneak behind her back anymore. She makes me happy. I hope that you can find someone that makes you just as happy as she has made me. She deserves better than what I am giving her. So I came here today to set healthy boundaries between you and I," Carl went on to say.

"Well, I figured that you had someone in your life, but I had no idea you were in a serious relationship," Amber responded with tears in her eyes. She was actually hoping that he was coming by to tell her that he wanted something more with her, but not this. She stood up from the kitchen table and removed her robe.

As she stood up, Carl's eyes bulged out of his head in surprise. He was mid-swallow when he noticed the growing belly that had previously been covered with that robe. Water spewed from his mouth as he choked on the discovery.

"I wanted to tell you, but you never seemed to have time to talk whenever I reached out, and this was not something I wanted to talk to you on the phone about. I felt that surely you would have come around before now," Amber explained.

"So you are saying that it's mine?!" Carl asked with grief in his voice.

"Yes. I am 18 weeks tomorrow," she replied.

"I don't know how I am going to explain this to Lynne!!! F**k!! How did I let this happen?!!" Carl screamed across the room as he plopped down on the couch in disgust.

"This was not a part of my plan. I do not want to become a father like this. Why did you wait so long to tell me? We could have done something about it before you got this far along. Lynne's going to leave me! I know she is!!" he went on to say as if Amber's feelings were a non-factor.

What Carl didn't know was that Lynne leaving him would be the exact outcome that Amber was hoping for. She wanted to be a family. She felt that having his child would make him see that she was the woman that he needed to settle down with. She didn't seem to care that Carl wasn't remotely in love with her.

Carl went home and contemplated how he would break the news to Lynne. He knew that this news could mean the end of their beautiful relationship. Either way, she had to know the truth. He sat down and told Lynne everything. Every detail, every time he and Amber had intercourse and even how they met. He explained that the only reason he found out about the pregnancy is because he went to break things off with Amber so that he could be completely faithful to her.

Lynne was crushed. This news definitely put a strain on their relationship, but surprisingly, Lynne understood the situation and chose to forgive Carl. She understood that Amber was going to be the mother of Carl's first child and had come to accept it.

Seeing that Lynne decided to stick things out with Carl after being so hurt by the pregnancy made Carl develop a whole different appreciation for Lynne. Carl continued to communicate with Amber, but with healthy boundaries in place.

After the birth of his son Carl Jr., Amber was reluctant about allowing Carl to come and get Junior, but she allowed it. She knew that having Carl come to get their son would ensure that she would have an opportunity to seduce him every time he came to get Junior or to drop him off. That was all she had working for her when it came to having Carl around. Carl only had eyes for Lynne, and Amber hated it.

Lynne seemed to have taken her role as step-mom with open arms. She went the extra mile when it came to Carl Jr. She loved the baby as if it were her own. Although the circumstances didn't turn out to be what Carl had planned when it came to having a happy family, having Carl Jr. around was as close to what he had envisioned as possible. He was ok with that.

Lynne's dedication and commitment to their relationship and now family convinced Carl that it was time to pop the big question. He wanted Lynne to carry his last name, to share the same name that his son carried. He popped the question, and Lynne was ecstatic. She said yes!

Carl didn't bother to tell Amber the news right away. He felt there was no need to rub it in her face. Things were peaceful, so the less she knew about his personal life, the better. The three of them had developed a routine when it came to Carl Jr. Lynne would step in to assist Carl whenever they would get him on the weekends and holidays. Amber was beginning to enjoy the freedom and benefits that came along with having Lynne around as well. She was like a free nanny to Amber. Whenever she wanted to plan something, she knew Lynne would always be ok with taking care of Junior if Carl was not available.

What Amber didn't know was Carl was planning on giving Lynne his last name. Several weeks before the wedding, as Carl was dropping Carl Jr. off to Amber's, he informed her that he would be getting married soon. Amber flipped out and told him, "Since you chose to marry her, you can kiss goodbye to ever seeing your child again!"

How Selfish...

He doesn't live here so he doesn't make decisions...

He Doesn't Live Here

*D*ebbie and Mark couldn't seem to see eye-to-eye on any decisions when it came to raising their son Tristan. After going back and forth for months with disagreements between the two of them, Debbie finally decided that whatever Mark had to say about her raising their son was no longer valid.

Debbie had begun dating a new love interest and Mark didn't like the idea of her bringing their son around strange men. Just two months prior, she had been dating someone else who she had brought around their son, and seeing as how that relationship did not last, Mark preferred that Debbie be in a serious relationship before introducing men to Tristan.

Debbie didn't seem to understand his logic whatsoever and felt that she should and could do whatever she wanted to.

This put a strain on the co-parenting relationship. Every time Mark made a suggestion on how things should be handled in regards to Tristan, Debbie's response was always, "He doesn't live here, so he doesn't make decisions."

How Selfish...

My husband is a better father than you

He's The Better Father

$\mathcal{B}$ryan was 26 years old and had recently re-enlisted for the next four years as a US Marine. His mother couldn't be more proud than she was right at that moment. Bryan was one of the smart ones that actually utilized every educational opportunity that came along with being in the military. As a child, Bryan loved football, and he had big dreams of being a star player someday. Bryan's dream of going off to play college football, however, was put on the backburner when he discovered that his high school sweetheart was pregnant two weeks after their high school graduation. With a child on the way, Bryan wanted to ensure that he was able to be a provider for his child, so he made the decision to sign up for the Marines. Seemingly so, he was on his second enlistment, and serving in the Marines had become his career.

The recruiter that encouraged him to join told him about all the benefits that came along with being in the military. He mentioned the housing, health benefits, educational resources, resources for the child that he had on the way, and the ability to live abroad with his now developing family. He weighed his options. Upon discovering that he would be receiving a paycheck with benefits on a consistent basis after his first three months in boot camp, he was sold. Signing up was not hypothetical anymore; it was a definite.

Bryan's decision rested solely on the fact that he was becoming a father, and he didn't want to be another statistic and have a son or daughter out in this world whose father didn't provide. Bryan was able to be there for the birth of his son, but it seemed like the longer he was in the military; the more he missed memorable moments.

Kim was Bryan's high school sweetheart, the mother of Bryan's son Kari. Kim had plans to go off to college immediately following her graduation to begin her journey in becoming the next big attorney in her family. Her mother and father owned their own firm; they had been pruning her to carry the family's legacy along with her brothers. She was determined that she, too, would make her parents proud and carry on the legacy.

Upon receiving the news of her unexpected and unplanned pregnancy, her family encouraged her not to keep the baby. With a successful future on the horizon, she would have her whole life to become a mother. The pregnancy could not have come at a worse time than right then; this is how Kim's family saw it.

Kim decided that keeping her child would be the only way that she could live with herself. Kim's parents advised her that if she kept her baby, the family would not support her. Her father insisted that Bryan would have to take care of her and the child from that point on. Blinded by love and a lack of knowledge of what being a parent consisted of, Kim did not see the financial obstacles that lay ahead.

Realizing that attending college upstate was no longer an option due to her pregnancy, she enrolled in a trade school to become a licensed cosmetologist. Her mother frowned upon her decision; working in a salon was something that was looked down upon by her elitist family. Although Kim had big dreams of becoming an attorney, she had always had a niche for hair and beauty. In high school, she was the go-to person for any girl that wanted to try a different look. The transition was a comfortable fit, however, her working hours allowed her less and less time to be home with Kari.

With the help that was coming from Bryan while he was away, Kim was able to obtain a small one-bedroom apartment for her and Kari. Having the financial support from Bryan was great, but the strain of not having his help physically was wearing down on Kim.

Kim's clientele was increasing by the day. Financially, she was doing quite well for herself. Despite what her parents thought about her decisions, she was determined to prove to them that she made the right decision. As a demand for her Custom Services increased, so did her working hours.

Kim envisioned owning her own business and began to put a plan in motion to open her own specialty service salon. With less time to have a personal life, Kim's life became a re-run of work and home on a daily basis. It seemed that every time Bryan tried to reach her, Kim was never available. With the lack of communication and feeling resentment from having to raise their son alone, it began to place a strain on their relationship.

Kim purchased her first three-bedroom townhome and was able to place Kari in the best Montessori Academy in her city. Considering the fact that she was now building her clientele, sometimes she would be required to work longer hours than the academy would run, so she hired Maria, the family nanny, to assist in getting Kari back and forth to school, preparing meals, completing laundry, and doing weekly home cleanings. With Maria's help, she did not seem to feel the strain of being a single parent as she had once before.

Maria's help allowed Kim the free time to enjoy her youth when she was not working. She began to connect with friends that she hadn't seen in years. As expected, most of her childhood girlfriends had married, or at least, secured a stable relationship. At times, being around her friends would be bittersweet, as she would hear them talk about the things that they would do with their significant others. She reflected on the fact that although she and Bryan were still technically together, she felt single.

She had not seen Bryan in months, their communication had become touch and go, and as Kari was getting older, she wanted more for him and more for herself. Just as she began the internal battle of deciding what would be the best thing to do in regards to her and Bryan's relationship, her phone rang. It was Bryan. She was happy that she was available to answer his call and catch up. Bryan was excited about his next adventure and could not wait to share the news with Kim.

Bryan informed Kim that he would be going to Okinawa, Japan, on a one-year deployment. He knew she wouldn't like the fact that, again, he would be gone on another extended stay, but with the increase in pay that he would receive for being overseas, he would be able to send her more financial assistance for her and their son.

Contrary to what Bryan thought, Kim could care less about the increase in her monthly stipend from him. Kim was only interested in knowing when they would be able to be a family like the one they had planned when he originally joined the military. This news caused her to question if there really was a future with Bryan. After all, she had been patiently waiting on him for years, and still, he had not even mentioned anything in regards to marrying her. What if she waited on him and he decided that she was not the woman that he wanted to marry? She didn't want to be the fool and be naive enough to think that it would be ok to continue to put her life on hold.

Bryan was approved to visit his family for the holidays, and Kim was eagerly awaiting his arrival. She had been thinking long and hard about her future, and she felt it was time for Bryan to piss or get off the pot! She decided that if Bryan would marry her, it would be worth waiting on him to finish his travels to Okinawa, Japan. He was scheduled to be home for 23 days and that was more than enough time for them to tie the knot before his deployment.

Kim did her research and discovered that because he was in active military, there was no waiting period for marriages; you could apply for your license and get married on the same day. Her only obstacle was that she had yet to discuss her plans with Bryan.

When Bryan arrived home, their chemistry was undeniable. Bryan was so happy to be able to have some bonding time with Kari. Kim planned a romantic date night for them and ensured that Maria was available for the remainder of the night. Things were going just as planned, and both Kim and Bryan were all smiles. They had done everything that she had planned, and Bryan was blown away with the amount of effort that went into planning such a memorable night. As their date was ending, Kim knew that it was time to speak to Bryan about their future.

Once they arrived to Kim's townhome, Bryan took the pleasure in tucking his son into bed. Kim waited for Bryan in the kitchen. As she stood at the sink, thinking of the best way to talk about such a sensitive topic, she worried that he would not want the same things that she did. She didn't know how Bryan felt about marriage, but it was time for her to find out.

Bryan approached her, wearing the same smile that caused Kim to fall in love with him years before.

"You've really outdone yourself tonight," said Bryan, as he approached Kim from behind while grasping the small of her waist.

"Anything for you, my love," she replied as she turned around to face Bryan. "I've been thinking about our future and I'd like to know what your plans are," she continued.

"What do you mean?" asked Bryan with a look of confusion.

"Your plans for us! Do you see yourself spending the rest of your life with me?" she asked him while staring directly into his eyes. Bryan was not ready for the questions that were coming from Kim's lips. He loved her without a doubt, but he was

38

not sure if marriage was something that he wanted to embark upon so young. Bryan wanted to be established as a man before taking that leap.

Sure, he managed to secure a career in the military, but there was so much that he wanted to experience out of life before locking himself down in a marriage. He never really had much of an opportunity to enjoy his youth since going straight to the military upon graduating high school. Although he and Kim shared a child together, it was purely circumstantial. Kari was not planned, but Bryan was going to do whatever it took to ensure that his son would be cared for. He could guarantee that the feelings he had in regards to caring for his son would not change, but with the time and distance that he had apart from Kim, marriage wasn't anywhere close to his thoughts.

"I love you Kim, but I haven't really given marriage much thought. There's still so much that I want to accomplish before getting married. Why all the questions about marriage anyway?" he asked in hopes that the conversation wouldn't actually continue.

"I wanted to know how you felt. I want more out of this relationship than just the child that we share. I want to be Mrs. Bryan Wells. I need the security of knowing that my waiting is not in vain. Plus, I looked into some things, and if we get married, you will receive an additional allowance, and the military will also provide us a home wherever you are stationed. We could finally be a family together," explained Kim.

Immediately, Bryan felt trapped. He had never questioned her pregnancy, or the fact that it happened unexpectedly. But should he? How could she possibly know this much information? He had never mentioned marriage benefits to her; she would have had to have someone in her ear. Did she see him as a meal ticket? Did she get pregnant because she knew that he had a full paid scholarship and was sure to go to the NFL if he would have stayed in school? Is that why she had been so patient about waiting on him all the times he had to serve thousands of miles away? Did she stay because her plan didn't work out and somehow she felt entitled to be his wife? His thoughts were consumed with questions.

The conversation did not end the way Kim was hoping for. For the remainder of his stay, he was very distant with Kim. He didn't want to end the relationship, he loved her; he just didn't want to get married by force. Unfortunately, Kim was trying to do just that: force his hand in marriage. Even though he was able to spend time with Kari, Kim's schedule made it quite convenient to avoid talking about what their plans would be moving forward. After all, there wasn't much more that he could do outside of all he had given up and provided.

Bryan was off to Japan, and Kim was left alone to raise Kari once again, with the exception of Maria's help. Since Bryan's visit, she spent countless hours thinking about what she would do concerning the uncertainty of a future with him. She concluded that although she and Bryan were still technically together, she would spend more time doing whatever made her happy and would let the chips fall wherever they may.

Several months later, as she waited for the valet to bring her car after attending girl's night out with her friends, she locked eyes with a familiar face. She immediately recognized him. It was Kenneth Brooks. She hadn't seen him since they were in middle school. All throughout Kim's elementary and middle school years, she and Kenneth's family were neighbors. Kim's parents moved to the suburbs her freshman year in high school.

Back when they were pre-teens, Kenneth wore a wired retainer, his pants never seemed to reach his ankles, and his crew consisted of the school's geek squad. Time had done him well. There he stood, 6'3, caramel complexion, well groomed, and rocking a tailored suit. His smile resembled a Colgate commercial: white, straight, and clean. He definitely had swag.

"Kim?" Kenneth asked as he began to walk toward her.

"Oh my God!! Kenneth Brooks!! It's been forever!" she shouted with excitement as she met him in his efforts to come her way. As she leaned in to give him a hug, she couldn't help but notice how good he smelled.

"It's me!" he replied as a huge smile came across his face.

"Girl whatever you have been doing, keep on doing it cause it's working for you. You look great!" he added, sliding in a compliment while meeting her embrace.

"Thank you, I do what I can until I can do what I want," she answered in a coy, yet feisty way. "Oh look, that's my car. It was really good to see you," she said as the valet stood holding the driver's door open for her.

"You aren't going to disappear on me again that easy. Is it ok that I call you? Perhaps you would let me treat you to lunch sometime?" Kenneth replied.

"Sure. I'd like that. Here's my card. That's my mobile number," she explained as she closed the clutch to her purse.

As she handed him the card, she said, "I look forward to it."

The following week while she was finishing her last client right before lunch, in walked Kenneth. He wasn't in a suit, but his ensemble was definitely tailored. Kim was caught off-guard by his surprise visit, but he had crossed her mind several times since the evening she waited for the valet, so she was happy to see him again.

"I'm sorry for coming to your job, but the card you gave me was somehow misplaced. I remembered the salon from the card, but I no longer had your number. I really wanted to keep in touch with you. I was wondering if you were available for lunch today? My treat," he said as he flashed his impeccable smile.

"Well sir, it must have been meant because I was actually about to go and grab me a bite to eat. I don't see why we can't eat together. What do you have in mind?" she asked, smiling back from ear to ear.

They went out to lunch that day, and every day after that for the next three weeks. Kim really liked Kenneth, but she and Bryan were still together. Kenneth was in complete awe when it came to Kim. He admired almost everything about her: the fact that she was a single mother trying to provide a better life for her son, and that she was working long hours with limited time for herself. She was very respectable and very open and honest about her relationship status with her son's father. Kenneth respected that, however, he was falling for this woman, so he relished in whatever time she was willing to set aside to spend with him.

After several months of spending time with Kenneth, she felt that what she was missing in Bryan, Kenneth could provide. She ended the relationship with Bryan, and things blossomed between her and Kenneth.

Kenneth had secured a prominent position as VP of Fidev Engineering and dedicated his free time to working with non-profit organizations that assisted single mothers. He had a soft spot for single mothers ever since his father and mother went through an ugly divorce.

Long before her and Bryan's breakup, she had started saving everything she could to invest in opening her own specialty salon. She had $30K of the $50K she needed. Kenneth saw her passion and discipline in regards to being so focused, so he wanted to help her bring her vision to fruition. For Kim's birthday, he surprised her with a *$20,000* cashier's check. She was floored. Although Bryan had done amazing things to help her, it was nothing in comparison to this.

After six months of being in a relationship, Kenneth proposed to Kim, and she gladly accepted. They married two months after the engagement. They were both successful as her specialty salon became one of the most popular salons in her area, and Kenneth still held the title of VP. Things were indeed moving fast, but Kim was happier than she had been in a long time, and that was all that mattered.

Kenneth and Kari became extremely attached to one another. The three of them were one big happy family.

Bryan couldn't believe that Kim had done him that way. He had given up a promising opportunity by sacrificing his football career so that she and Kari could be taken care of when her parents decided to turn their backs on her, and this is how she repaid him? He was hurt. He had already been accustomed to the distance and time away from Kim and Kari, so it gave him no choice but to accept everything for what it was.

Kim had made it very clear that she wanted to get married, and Bryan had made it clear that he wasn't entertaining those thoughts anytime soon. Bryan did have a problem understanding how she could marry a man that she had dated less than a year. He was concerned about the type of man she was bringing around his son, the son that he had sacrificed his dream to protect.

Bryan felt helpless, knowing that another man was getting the time with his son that he so desperately craved. He hadn't even had an opportunity to meet the man that he was almost sure his son was calling daddy in his absence.

44

With the passing of time, the idea of Kim moving on and getting married no longer bothered him. However, he worried for his son frequently because of the concerns of bringing a stranger around.

Bryan was able to return home after his year of staying overseas and called Kim to let her know that he would be in town in two weeks for a week before relocating to San Diego to report for duty.

"Hello," Kim said as she answered the phone.

"What's up Kim? How's Kari? How are you?" Bryan asked.

"Hi Bryan, we're great. Kari is doing so well. Kenneth enrolled him in Tae Kwon Do. You should see him, he's so cute in his uniform," she answered, without realizing that Bryan didn't ask about Kenneth for a reason; he didn't call to discuss Kenneth.

"I'll see soon enough!" he replied with a chuckle in his voice. "I'll be there in two weeks for a week and I wanted to come by and pick up Kari for the week that I am in town."

"I will have to get back to you on that. I need to discuss that with Kenneth, and I'll let you know," she answered.

"What in the hell does Kenneth have to do with me seeing my son?!" he yelled into the phone. He had always tried to be pleasant when it came to dealings with his son, knowing that he was so far away. But hearing Kim place Kenneth's concerns before his was gut wrenching. At that moment, his smile was quickly erased.

"You may be Kari's dad, but Kenneth is here being his father. He is the one taking him to practice and teaching him things he should know as a young boy. Did you know I was allowing him to sit down to pee? I didn't even know there was a problem with that?" she continued sarcastically.

"Again, what does any of that have to do with me coming to get my son?" he asked with a tone of frustration. "I am his father! I take damn good care of my son!"

Before he could get out another word, Kim quickly interrupted and said, "I don't want to argue about it. Like I said, I will talk to Kenneth about it and let you know if he can go. You can't be upset with me because my husband is a better father than you!"

Bryan was enraged at Kim's response. How could someone else have more authority over his son than him after all he had sacrificed? Even though he was provoked about her even mentioning that she would have to speak to him first, the mere fact that she had the nerve to tell him that Kenneth was a better father than he was, after all he'd done for them, hurt him to the core.

Nope
I sure
Didn't answer
The door
For his
Weekend

Can't Have Her Way

"*Hey* Tara, it's Cedric. I am at your front door. Can you pick up your phone? I don't know what's going on. You knew I was on my way. I can see that you're home, so stop playing around," Cedric said as he hit the end button on his cell phone. He had been standing there for ten minutes already and with every second that passed, his frustration was becoming more intense.

After calling Tara two more times, he decided that he would just leave and try reaching Tara later to find out why she refused to open the door.

Tara knew he was standing there, but she wanted to teach him a lesson. Earlier that week, Tara asked Cedric if he could help her get her car out of the shop and to her surprise, he told her 'No'.

Back when they were married, Cedric would do any and everything for Tara. She was the definition of *spoiled.* Since their divorce, he had still remained consistent in taking care of her personal needs if he saw that it would be beneficial to their daughter. But since he and his new fiancé had moved in together, he had not been as attentive to the needs of his ex-wife. His focus had been on building a future with his soon-to-be wife instead.

Cedric had no problem helping when it was needed, but the way he saw it, if she really felt like getting her car fixed was a priority, she wouldn't be planning to go to Miami the following weekend.

Instead, she would spend that money to get her car fixed. Needless to say, Tara was not happy with Cedric's response and convinced herself that his fiancé must have been the reason behind him not helping her.

At that moment, Tara decided that she didn't want her daughter around Tiffany, Cedric's fiancé. At least that was the excuse that she would use. So when Cedric arrived to get their 4-year-old daughter Janay, Tara didn't open the door. She felt like she really didn't owe him an explanation.

"He didn't explain to me why he couldn't get my car out of the shop; I don't need to explain why I am not opening the door.", Tara thought to herself.

As Tara stood peeking out the window as Cedric drove away, Stacey, Tara's best friend, stood there with a puzzled look on her face. She, too, thought that Janay surely was going with her dad. Just before Cedric had arrived, Stacey's cell phone rang, so she went to the backroom to have her conversation in privacy. She figured with the time that she had spent in the other room that she would have missed her chance to kiss Janay goodbye. Instead, Janay was sitting in the living room, still in her play clothes.

"What's up Tara? I thought Janay was going with her dad this weekend?" Stacey asked, still maintaining a puzzled look.

"She was supposed to, but he is tripping so I'm going to teach him to tell me what he's not going to do when I ask him to do something.", Tara replied with an attitude.

"Aww girl, I was going to ask you if you wanted to go to karaoke with me since you weren't going to have the baby," Stacy explained.

"That won't be a problem, I can just call her nanny to come and spend the night," Tara replied.

"Well, isn't this his weekend anyway?" Stacey asked. Stacey couldn't understand why Tara would not let Janay go with her father instead. That way, she wouldn't have to hire a nanny, and she would have the entire weekend instead of just the night.

As stubborn as Tara was, she knew that the only way to get under Cedric's skin would be through their daughter. He might not do anything for her anymore, but he'd do anything for his daughter, and Tara used their child to her advantage *and* against him whenever she didn't get her way.

How Selfish...

*

* *

I will keep
Increasing
Child support
Because
I need to pay
My bills

* *

*

Treated Like a Thief

BD: Hey my family is having their reunion in a few weeks, and I really want to take our daughter, but it's not my weekend. Can we switch weekends or can I get her two weekends in a row?

BM: Where is the family reunion?

BD: Out of state in Louisiana.

BM: I am not comfortable with you leaving the state with her.

BD: I can give you the address, so you will know where we are exactly.

BM: Let me think about it.

BD: Think about what?

BM: I need to think about if I am okay with her going.

BD: I am her father, so what is there to discuss? I pick her up and drop her off on time, and I pay child support and health insurance. Besides, whenever you need something, I give it to you.

BM: Again, let me think about it.

Call the school
Again trying to run
Stuff I will
Take you back to
Court and request
More money!

You Shouldn't Have Left

$\mathcal{T}$aria was self-absorbed in every way you could imagine, and if things didn't go her way, there was always a problem. This caused many people to grow a significant dislike for her abrasive personality; it also drove her ex-fiancé Kevin away.

She literally made Kevin's life miserable. She would provoke him into anger and play the victim every chance she got. This created an unhealthy environment for everyone, so eventually Kevin decided that it was best that they end the relationship and focus on their daughter.

Kevin was the father of Taria's six year-old daughter, however he rarely received the chance to see her because Taria would go strictly by the guidelines of an every other weekend visitation. Kevin's off days were always unpredictable because the company he worked for only allowed him one weekend off a month; all other weekends were mandatory for him.

This left Kevin in a complicated situation. He tried to find another job, but finding one that could match what he was bringing home was a challenge. With the eight hundred a month he was giving Taria for child support, taking a lesser-paying job just to have weekends off with his daughter was almost impossible for him.

When Kevin tried to explain his dilemma to Taria, the only thing she had to say in return was, "That is not my problem. You shouldn't have left."

It's apparent that Taria doesn't realize the damage that she is causing in her daughter's relationship with her father. He has asked to be able to pick her up from school on all the days he doesn't work, but Taria insists on making it difficult for him to see his daughter.

How Selfish...

Your Weekend, Your Problem

BD: Hey I wanted to talk to you about switching weekends. I have to work on the 1st and 3rd weekends of the month.

BM: You need to find someone to take care of our child on your weekends.

BD: Why should I have to do that?

BM: Because that is your assigned weekend.

BD: What is the point of picking up our child if we can't bond or spend time together?

BM: Well that is your problem.

BD: I just got this job. There is no way they will let me switch weekends.

BM: Again, that is not my problem.

*

***

Send your
Wife over
Here again
And she won't
Leave with our
Child

***

*

Your Mom Doesn't Run Things

BD: Hey my mother wants to come by and pick up Samiya to spend the weekend with her.

BM: Why can't she come on your weekend and get her?

BD: She is visiting this weekend from Virginia and will only be in Texas for four days.

BM: She should have arranged her trip around your weekend. Your mother is always doing things on her own and not talking to anyone as if she's running things. So, tell your mother she can enjoy looking at the pictures because I'm not budging!

BD: Don't disrespect my mother. She doesn't know anything about the court ordered paperwork. She simply just wanted to fly down here to visit her granddaughter and me.

BM: Tell your mom the next time she plans a trip that she needs to check with you to see if it's your weekend. Your mother's travel plans are not my problem.

If the child lives with the father 90% of the time and visits the mother 10% of the time, should decisions be 50/50 between father and mother?

Vindictive Actions

$\mathcal{T}$here is nothing worse than a woman that's out to get you! Here we have Audrey, a mother who is determined to make her baby daddy pay one way or another, even if it means jail time. Unfortunately for Thomas, Audrey wasn't his only baby mama that felt this way. It seems that Monica, Tera and Patricia all had the same sentiments... Yep! You guessed it! Thomas had 4 baby mamas.

For years, none of the other baby mamas cared much for Audrey since wherever Audrey went, drama was sure to follow. After Thomas and Audrey's break-up, Thomas got engaged to a successful actress, and they began sharing a condo together. The newfound information sent Audrey into an obsession that you wouldn't believe. Audrey started finding new ways to bring complications into Thomas's household, from drama on social media to being disrespectful when dropping off their daughter to family functions of Thomas's. It seemed that the problems were never ending in Thomas's life when it came to her.

Since moving in with his fiancé, Thomas had not given much attention to all of Audrey's shenanigans. Thomas felt that not giving her the attention that she so badly craved would eventually cause her to tire, and she would move on with her life instead of bringing so much drama to his. So Thomas stopped answering her calls, and only responded to texts that had something to do with their daughter. There was no way of communicating with this woman, not healthy communication anyway.

She'd insult him and degrade him as a man, then play the victim every time she was in the wrong. To make matters worse, she'd call around to friends and family and further cause insult to injury by embellishing on her side of the story. The best thing that Thomas felt he could do with Audrey was to cut communication with her and allow all of their differences to be settled in court. Besides, Thomas was paying Audrey the mandated child-support as ordered and had visitation arrangements already determined by the court. As far as Thomas was concerned, as long as he was able to see his daughter, Audrey could run tell the *President* her side of the story, and it wouldn't cause Thomas to lose one minute of sleep!

Anyone that was privy to coming into contact with Audrey and getting to know her grew a clear understanding that Audrey was a master manipulator. Although Thomas had three other baby mamas, Audrey was the only one that had placed him on child support. Thomas had developed an understanding with the mothers of his other children that whenever the child needed something that they could just call him and he'd deliver. So far, this seemed to be working out well for everyone.

There was no doubt that Thomas had left a sour taste in the mouths of his baby mamas due to the fact that their relationships never resulted into the happy family that each of them had envisioned. But one thing they couldn't say was that he didn't take care of his kids. He didn't always send those women a set amount every month, but he definitely made sure that he would provide when asked.

Audrey decided that it was time to make things interesting. She reached out to Monica, Tera and Patricia under the guise that she wanted to get all four of the children together, so they could build relationships with one another. With an excuse like that, it was easy bait. Before you knew it, all four ladies started meeting on Saturday mornings to let the kids play at the outdoor water park. They even made a pact that Thomas wouldn't know or be invited, as this was something that they all wanted for their children: to know their siblings. The other ladies weren't very sure what all the secrecy was about, but decided there was no harm in it either way. Besides, it was nothing more than allowing the kids to bond with one another.

By the third Saturday, all the ladies had begun to warm up to one another. Audrey didn't seem so bad. She came off as a concerned mother that only wanted the best for her daughter and her daughter's siblings. Somehow, the topic of school shopping came up as one of the other mothers talked about her plans for the day. This was the perfect opportunity for Audrey to put her plan in motion!!

"I hope you are getting Thomas to help you out with your school shopping!" said Audrey as Patricia broke down her shopping plans for the day.

"He always does. It may not be much, but he does something every year," explained Patricia.

"You too?" asked Tera.

"Well we alternate," Monica interrupted.

"Alternate? What do you mean by that?" Tera asked, with a look of confusion.

Monica began to explain, "Well if he covers Christmas, I cover the school shopping and vice versa. We switch it up every year."

"Well, I don't have those problems. My princess is well taken care of, and you all could be getting a whole lot more than what he's giving you. I can't believe that you ladies are carrying the majority of the load while he lives it up with Little Miss Actress. I went to the child support office, and I was told that based on his income and having four children that we each could get $500 a month in child support, and he would have to provide medical insurance. I don't know about you all, but that extra $6,000 a year in guaranteed support along with medical insurance sounds a lot better than having to call him and ask him for money every time our daughter needs something or is sick," explained Audrey.

Audrey was only getting $300 a month, but in order to encourage the other mothers to follow suit, she had to make the deal sweeter.

"$500 A MONTH?!!!" Monica interrupted.

"Yes Ma'am. The Attorney General's office knows how much he makes and determines the amount he should pay based on the amount of money he makes and the number of children he has. So I suggest you ladies stop short-changing yourselves and get the help from him that you deserve instead of just taking the crumbs he has left over," replied Audrey.

"Makes a lot of sense," Patricia said under her breath as the group of ladies received this revelation coming from Audrey.

To make it even more convincing, Audrey had to add, "Speaking of Little Miss Actress, did you see the pictures they posted on Facebook from their trip to the Bahamas?"

"Girl, No!!! Must be nice!" Tera said, with sarcasm in her voice.

"It is! And guess who else is taking trips now? Me and my baby! Thomas won't be the only one enjoying his life, and with the child support that I receive, I can now afford to take my baby girl on trips as well. I'm trying to tell y'all, don't cheat yourself, treat yourself. Your kids deserve the finer things too, and you did not make those babies by yourselves. I say make him step up to the plate and stop waiting on crumbs!" Audrey replied.

Obviously, Audrey's plan worked! The following week, the other three ladies made an appointment with the Attorney General's Office to file for child support. Audrey had achieved the outcome that she was looking for by having all the other mothers of Thomas's children go to file cases against him, even though he was doing his part as a father. This made things very difficult for him, even to the point where he and his fiancé had to give up their condo until he could hire an attorney to get a modification done on the child support payments.

How Selfish...

She Called the Police

BM: Where are you?

BD: I got caught up in traffic, but I should be there in about 30 minutes.

BM: You should have left earlier because I told you to have her here on time.

BD: Sometimes things happen, and you and I both know that I have no control over traffic.

BM: Well let me go ahead and call the police because this needs to be documented.

BD: Are you serious?

BM: You're probably lying and had my baby over there with your girlfriend, but whatever bye!

*

***

He has custody so I pay child support. Why is it that I have to pay child support, but I am not allowed to request receipts for what he is spending the money on?

***

*

On Her Time Only

$\mathcal{A}$s a father, I try to do my best and really be there for my two sons. My baby mama makes this hard for me, especially since the divorce. When the two of us were married, we followed a strict schedule for academics and recreation. Mondays, Wednesdays, and Fridays were my days for homework and recreation. Tuesdays and Thursdays, I would take the responsibility of cleaning and cooking after work.

We talked about everything before we officially divorced. She informed me we could still follow the same routine. I could still have Mondays, Wednesdays, and Fridays, but I had to have the kids home by 10:00p.m. for bedtime; I totally understood this. Since I was no longer doing Tuesdays and Thursday's cleaning and cooking at home, I worked it out with my boss to go into work early on Mondays, Wednesdays and Fridays, so I could get off and cook dinner for my kids before picking them up from daycare at 5:00p.m.

We finally came to some decisions involving the house and other joint-owned items, and the divorce was final. I was so happy to be separated from her, but not from my kids. We went to court on a Wednesday to hear the final verdict. I immediately called her, so I could get the kids like we discussed. She told me that she didn't know because she wanted to explain to the kids that week how the changes were going to be. Instead of making a fuss about it, I was understanding. The following weekend wasn't my scheduled weekend, so I didn't bother with trying to get the kids.

I called her Sunday to let her know that I would pick them up from daycare at 5:00p.m. the next day. I asked her if she needed me to pick up anything for the kids at home, and I could make sure it got done before I dropped them off at 10:00p.m.

She told me she was not feeling the arrangement and didn't want them feeling like they were growing up in two homes. Keep in mind, I didn't get the visitations court-ordered because we had already discussed our arrangements and seemed to agree on them, so I didn't feel the need to do that. Now I wish I did. After battling for weeks and months, I am only allowed to follow the court-ordered visitation schedule of every other weekend and a few hours during the week. I can't believe she did me this way; she knows how I feel about my kids.

No Invite

$\mathscr{D}$estiny always comes to visit me every other weekend. I wish she could come every weekend, but her mother only wants to follow the legal documents from the Attorney General's office.

One weekend, my Destiny came to visit from Friday to Sunday, and around 10 AM Sunday morning, her mother called telling me she had to come home early to go to a birthday party. She further went on to ask me to have her ready by noon.

Destiny is only five years old, so of course, I don't want her to miss any parties or functions to be with friends. I gave my little princess a kiss goodbye and looked forward to seeing her in a few weeks.

When she came to visit me two weeks later, she gave me a picture from a play she was in the previous month. When I looked at the pictures, I noticed the date at the bottom was the Sunday her mother had called asking for her to be picked up early for a birthday party.

When I asked Destiny about it, she said she was in a play at a theatre. I was so upset that I was not told anything about my baby being in a play. So I called her mother and asked her why did she choose not to mention anything about it when she called to pick Destiny up early during my scheduled visitation. I wanted to know why she felt I didn't need to be there.

"Because you wasn't invited. That is why you weren't notified," she said with sarcasm. I just hung up the phone. Since when do I need an invitation as her father to attend events my little one is participating in?

* *

Every other
weekend when she
goes off with her
father, I send her
in old clothes so I
can get new
clothes sent back.
* *

Divorced and Still a Headache

$\mathcal{My}$ name is Dwight and I am a stressed baby daddy...

The bright sun greets me every morning as I rise from the bed on which I hover with sadness from not having my Saraj here. Saraj is my only child, my heartbeat and the reason I live and breathe. Every Friday, I make it a point to leave work earlier than normal to pick Saraj up from school at 2:15pm.

Whenever I arrive, the school calls her mother Debra, because I am not on the list for daily pick-ups. The process is long, irritating and painful because she purposely doesn't answer the phone which means I have to sit and wait until she gives the okay. As the biological father, some things I feel I shouldn't have to go through.

It seems that she gets a kick out of diminishing my manhood in front of others. Whenever my daughter and I go about our weekends of laughter and unity, her mother calls her cell phone every few hours just to speak with her. In the past, I would take the cell phone during our time together and express to Saraj's mother to call my phone if she needed to speak with her, instead of continuously interrupting father-daughter time.

After I did that, Debra took me to court and expressed to the judge the importance of Saraj having a cell phone for family emergencies.

As Saraj's father, I told the judge I would never disagree with my ex-wife's expressions, but I didn't see the reasoning behind calling multiple times within the day. Forcing Saraj to answer her phone while walking out the movie theatre, or three calls during two hours of a scheduled movie production seemed unfair when it was not an emergency.

The courts ruled in Debra's favor as always. Debra really abused the system to continuously torture and bother me with her level of control. Oh yeah, I forgot to mention visitation was placed on hold until the visitation hearing took place. Not only did I have to wait to see Saraj for two months, but Debra changed her number so I wasn't able to speak with her at all during the two-month period.

After the court hearing, Debra approached me and said, "You just insist on wanting control, and wanting control is fine, but in the end this is what happens when you leave your family. Deal with it."

Debra and I were married for 7 years; we argued on a daily basis about the same situations and scenarios. Saraj was born 2 years into the marriage. As a man who grew up in a home filled with domestic violence, I decided it would not be wise to raise Saraj in an unhealthy environment, so I left. Since I left, Debra has been sticking it to me.

I consider myself to be a man. I pay my child support, and whenever she calls my phone for money separate from child support, I place it in her hand, but she gives me no respect. I would like to see my Saraj every day or three days each week, but when I ask to see her, I get told 'no', or my phone calls get ignored. Disappearing just seems to be the best thing to do for peace of mind. I am so sick of Debra and her selfish ways.

If the child lives with the father 90% of the time and visits the mother 10% of the time, and he still pays child support, is that fair?

Baby Mama Drama

My baby mama, Janice, was someone I met years back. We never dated, but engaged in casual intercourse from time to time. From this careless behavior, we gave birth to a beautiful boy, Simon. Having a child out of wedlock is really shunned in my family. My father is a Pastor, and my mother is the head member over the weekly Bible study. When my parents heard the news, they were devastated.

Making it work as a family with Janice was not a priority of mine and dealing with her on a daily basis was not on the list. The first few years were truly hard since the two of us lived in separate homes. The battles were intense, the arguments were fierce, the choice of curse words cut like knives, and the hostility was obvious to all family members and friends.

I realized my time was being wasted going back and forth with Janice. It was time that I stopped the perpetual cycle and moved on to find someone more compatible to be with.

One day, while at a BBQ, I met Aisha, the woman I knew I was going to marry. She was sweet and coy. Everything about her screamed *lady-like*. During my first 6 months of dating Aisha, I had spoken with my mother and asked her if she would pick up Simon and bring him to the house instead of me going to Janice's myself.

I did this to keep my mind at peace and really focus on dating Aisha. My son never met Aisha until after I proposed to her. Once I solidified my engagement, I started picking up Simon again.

On several occasions, Janice came to the door and expressed how she felt I was not a man and that I was a coward. The old me would have said some disgusting words, and my face would have glowed with anger, but I was not going to go there with her. I hoped the war between us would end if one of us stayed silent and level headed.

I didn't tell Janice about the engagement, but it wasn't long before Simon went home and told her. As Simon's father, I wanted to tell Janice, but I wanted to do it by taking Janice and Aisha to dinner. I do not fault my Simon for telling his mother. Knowing his mother, she grilled him for hours to get the information.

Janice called me, and the griping began. Her insults coupled with the annoying tone of her voice always had a way of raising my blood pressure. Instead of arguing with her, I replied, "You're right and we can discuss another time."

Janice gives me a migraine. One weekend, I called Janice to let her know I would be dropping Simon back home a few hours earlier on the following Sunday. Janice informed me that it was okay, and bringing Simon home early wasn't a problem. The calmness in her voice without the addition of insulting phrases was a true shock. Instead of questioning her about it, I accepted it as progress.

When Aisha, Simon and I pulled up to the driveway, Simon got out the car to walk to the door. He knocked and knocked, and there was no answer. I called Janice to see if she was in the house and to see if she was okay. No answer. She pulled up a whole hour later, and of course, my fiancé was upset because we were headed to a concert and we were late.

When Janice pulled up, I asked her what was the deal. She said, "I don't know what you are talking about."

I looked at her and just wanted to shake her. I said to Janice, "I spoke with you earlier this week to let you know I was bringing Simon home a few hours early because I had something to do. You said okay as in that was cool."

Janice didn't waste any time letting me know she was not on my schedule and she didn't have to answer to me. My soul was so tired of her acting silly I was about to explode. Before I could do this, Aisha yelled my name, asking me to come to the car and be done with the conversation.

Instead of Janice allowing me to walk away, she approached Aisha in the passenger seat to tell her that minding her business would be a great idea. Of course Aisha was not going to argue with her, so she let the window up. Janice came back and followed me to the car. As I tried to hurry to the car to avoid further confrontation or making a scene in front of her neighbors, she began pushing and shoving me. After her rant, she finally went back into the house with Simon.

Not only did we have an argument in front of our son, she also pushed me in front of my son. Too much drama.

She Abducted My Kids

*W*hen I met my wife, I fell so hard and only wanted her. We decided to get married, and she let me know she wanted to have many babies from me. After five years of marriage, we gave birth to two beautiful boys. Life was good at first, but eventually, everything went downhill. We started arguing more often than not, and it seemed nothing I did would make her happy.

I suggested counseling, and she agreed, so we went together. When we were talking to the counselor, she told him that she felt I was setting her up to lock her down with children. Instead of getting upset, I reminded her of our previous discussions about her wanting to have many children together.

As the counselor was listening, she suggested that my wife be evaluated for depression. The doctor asked her questions and concluded she was clinically depressed. She refused to take the medicine prescribed, so every day was so hard for the boys and I.

The Super Bowl was approaching, and the fellas had planned a trip. I was stoked to be able to go. I told my wife that taking a trip out of town would be a much-needed break. She understood. I was not going to give up on my wife; I just needed a few days alone, without all of the arguing.

When I arrived back from Super Bowl weekend that Monday morning, my wife and kids were not home. I wasn't worried about it because she would always go to the store on Monday mornings. I waited for two hours for them to come home, and then I started to get worried. I called her cell phone, and it was disconnected. That was a shock because my cell phone wasn't disconnected.

I called the cell phone company, and they told me she canceled the phone line and reported the phone lost Sunday night. I really was shocked because she never told me that and I had talked to her Monday morning on the home phone before getting on my flight. I looked at the clock. It was close to 3:00p.m. and still no show from my wife or kids. I decided to call her mom and see if she was over there.

My wife's mother let me know that she hadn't talked to her since Sunday morning. Time passed and before I knew it, it was 6:03p.m. I became really worried. I decided to call the police and file a report. Since we were married and I had spoken with her that morning, they couldn't process the missing person complaint until they were missing 48 hours. I went back to the police department exactly 48 hours later and filed the report.

I called all her friends and family, and no one had seen or talked to her since that Sunday morning. Seven years later, still no show from my wife and kids. I didn't have the money to search for them or even afford a lawyer, and I still have no idea where my wife and kids are.

Ball Player Blues

$\mathcal{I}$ worked hard all my life. I played basketball in elementary and middle school, was the star player in high school, and received a full scholarship to one of the top colleges to play ball. Before getting drafted to the NBA, I was married. My ex-wife gave birth to two boys. She held me down, but I wasn't really fond of someone like her on my arm. She was cute, but she had her issues. I wanted a high-class woman that had goals and ambitions. All she wanted to do was sit at home, watch TV, and go out with her friends.

I realized that we had our children young, so it wasn't unheard of for people our age to go out. The problem was that her behavior became persistent. No matter how much I tried to encourage her to be more productive, her habits became consistent. She developed bad eating habits, she stopped working out, and she became more and more hostile every time she didn't get her way. She was just a "stressful situation" all the time.

Whenever she wanted to blame me for why she didn't pursue her dreams, it would lead to more arguments, so I filed for divorce. Later, I went off to the NBA.

While I was in the NBA, I met a woman who changed my life. She was older than I, but she was so beautiful. We had a great relationship and blended well. We dated for about a year until I could finalize my divorce. Once my divorce was finalized, we were married six months later.

She was unable to have children naturally, so we had to do a medical procedure. From this, she gave birth to twin boys. We moved into a 10-bedroom home, and life was good. What was mine was hers and what was hers was mine.

Once she gave birth to our children, she started acting differently. I wasn't around much because I was playing basketball, and it required me to make many appearances. This is what kept the bills paid and provided my wife with any and everything she wanted. Before we married, she signed a prenuptial agreement, but this did not mess up our relationship.

Eventually, she started seeing me on the internet in photos with women. This would cause many unnecessary conversations. I continued to explain to her that those women were "groupics". Everyone knows 'groupies' get excited when they see ball players. I know many ball players are cheaters and disloyal to their wives, but that was not the case for me. I tried to reassure her that my heart was there with her, but she let her insecurities diminish any trust that I thought we had built.

Since she did not like having to see me on social media and websites with other women, she filed for divorce. I didn't want to divorce my wife, but I was never a man to keep a woman that doesn't want to be kept. She gave me ultimatums that were beyond my control. It was either tell my fans no to picture requests, or divorce her. There was no happy median when it came to her. I couldn't do that to the people who would come to my games holding up my jersey. So I had to let her do what made her happy. I was ok, knowing I had done nothing but provide a good lifestyle for her and our sons.

Since she signed a prenuptial agreement, she wasn't able to get anything from me but the house.

Having a set of twins, though, she was able to get a high amount of child support. What I didn't know was she had started taking money out of the account while she was married to me and was planning to divorce me all along.

She purchased a home in Italy and moved there after the divorce. She knows I'm a basketball player who travels within the states most of the year. I couldn't understand why she would move into a home in Italy.

She fought for sole custody, and she won the case because she kept a log of the days I was actually in town. She felt that as their father, I could fly to Italy to see them during my off-season since that is what I was doing while married.

It seems that the mothers of my children are the complete opposite from one another, but both of them managed to leave a sour taste in my mouth when it comes to having more children. Why do they have to be so selfish?

Favoritism

$\mathcal{I}$have two kids with my ex-wife, and it is a hassle trying to pick them up every other weekend, even seeing them during the week. She makes it really hard for a father like myself. One weekend, I picked up my baby boy and baby girl, and we went to Chuckie Cheese to have a blast. When they were sitting in the backseat of the car, I overheard my babies talking, and my son told his sister, "I am really tired of doing all the cleaning and housework. Mom doesn't make you do anything. She lets you sit around and watch TV all day."

Instead of interrupting their conversation, I decided to drop them off and ask their mother about it. She replied, "Our daughter is a princess and I want her to always feel like one."

Our son is a boy that will one day be a man, and she felt like he needed to know how to do house chores. When we were married, I made her feel like a housewife. As a result, she didn't want our son to be like me: bossy and controlling.

"That is all well and good, but if you don't allow our daughter to be taught the same principles, that itself is so wrong on so many levels," I replied.

She told me I had myself to thank for this situation, and life goes on. She also informed me, 'this is what happens when you abandon your family'. I told her I didn't abandon them. I had to remind her that she came to me and told me she didn't want to be married anymore, so I chose to grant her what she wanted.

So when my daughter came over for my weekends, I made sure I started teaching her along with her brother to keep everything clean. I only allowed for one hour of clean up time. Our babies went back home and told their mother what I would do on my weekends. Since they told her that I give both of them an equal share of responsibility, she hasn't sent our daughter on weekends anymore, only our son.

How selfish can you be?

Confession:

Therapist: Do you feel you are a bad mother?

BM: No, I am not. But I will admit that I would do anything to make my child's father suffer for not wanting to marry me and be a family.

Therapist: Don't you feel that is a bit deceiving and mean to do to your child's father?

BM: Yes, but men do it all the time, and I am tired of men, especially my child's father, treating me with disrespect.

Therapist: You don't think the games you play are disrespectful, mean, or deceiving?

BM: I know it's not right, but I haven't gotten anywhere by being nice and "playing by the rules". Playing by the rules gets me no love or respect. The other women who don't deserve it get all the love and respect.

Therapist: You and your child's father have to encounter each other for the rest of your lives. How do you think your child will be affected by this?

BM: I am doing the best I can and can't worry about that.

Bitter Baby Mama

$\mathcal{T}$hings seemed to be going smoothly between Timothy and his ex-wife Samantha after a year of drama-filled occurrences. Samantha blamed Timothy for all the wrong things that had occurred in her life since the divorce. Topped with the fact that the two divorced shortly after the birth of their child, Samantha couldn't seem to do the two things that seemed to consume her the most...keep a relationship or lose that extra 60lbs she had gained. This caused a bitterness inside her that made it hard for others to take a liking to her as a person.

Timothy and Samantha shared a handsome little boy. This was the couple's only child together. Although Timothy had other children from other women, this was his first son. That alone caused a bond between Timothy and his son that you could not imagine. Even though Timothy and Samantha did not work out as a couple, Timothy was determined not to let that get in the way of him being a part of Bashari's life.

After the divorce, Timothy reunited with his old high school sweetheart, Charlotte, and they were married a year after. This did not go over very easily with Samantha, and it wasn't long before Samantha started using Bashari as a pawn to control things in Timothy's home. Samantha didn't hold any reservations when it came to expressing how she felt about Timothy's new marriage. She would make it a point to set up the pickups and drop offs, demanding that Charlotte not be around for the exchange.

However, Samantha was the Queen of manipulation because she would pretend to like Charlotte whenever it was convenient for her. There was a time she wanted to go out of town on a Women's Retreat, and Timothy was working out of town and unavailable, Samantha seemed to have no problems with Charlotte. She even came across quite friendly when it was time to drop Bashari off at Charlotte and Tim's home.

After some time, Samantha had begun allowing Timothy to have Bashari on a regular basis again, sometimes a week at a time on an unscheduled visitation. Timothy's new wife Charlotte began to develop her own bond with Bashari. She cared for him as her very own. Charlotte was not new to the mothering experience as she raised three children of her own. Whenever Basahri would come over, Charlotte's motherly instincts would kick right in.

Charlotte was sure to prepare home-cooked, healthy, wholesome meals for Bashari, keep him on a great schedule for nap, bath and bedtime, and even do story time before bed. There was nothing that Charlotte would not do for little Bashari and Timothy loved her more for that.

Samantha had been planning Bashari's third birthday party for well over a month, and it was approaching fast. She sent Timothy a text message with all of the details for the party. Considering that Samantha had been sending Bashari to his father's more often than usual, and Charlotte had been stepping in to assist in the care of Bashari, even in

Timothy's absence, Timothy didn't hesitate to share the invite and info with his current wife, Charlotte...

Day of the Party...

Samantha had planned a huge birthday event for Bashari's 3rd Birthday at Main Event Indoor Arcade and Theme Park. She sent invites to all of her friends and family as well as Timothy's friends and family members. She wanted Bashari to be surrounded by all of his family and loved ones. At least, this is what she told Timothy's mother when she sent her the invite. This came to a surprise to everyone since Samantha had been so disrespectful to Bashari's grandmother on numerous occasions. Nevertheless, Gi-Gi was not going to miss her grandson's birthday party.

As Samantha was posing for a picture with her sister and son, her bright smile was quickly replaced by a grim scowl as she looked off into the distance towards the entrance.

In walked Timothy and Charlotte, all smiles, with gift bags in tote. Bashari noticed them and began to run towards them in excitement.

"Cee-Cee! Cee Cee!" shouted Bashari as he made eye contact with Charlotte. Cee-Cee was what he called her for short.

Before Bashari could reach his dad and step-mom, Samantha grabbed him by his arm and signaled for him to sit down. Samantha began shouting over the crowd, "Why did you bring her here! Get that b***h out of my baby's birthday party!" Both Timothy and Charlotte froze in their tracks at this outburst. Timothy was never one for

90

drama and always took the peaceful road in situations; this was one of those situations where he just wanted to do just that. In most cases, Charlotte took the same approach.

As Timothy reached towards Charlotte suggesting that it was time to go, he calmly said, "C'mon babe, let them have their day. We'll throw him a party ourselves next year."

He turned towards the door, but this was the last straw for Charlotte. She had been disrespected by Samantha for the last time. Although she didn't want to contribute to ruining Bashari's birthday party, she knew that something had to be said.

Charlotte turned sharply away from Timothy in Samantha's direction and replied. "You know what? Normally I'd let you make it, but enough is enough! You mean to tell me that you can drop him off for weeks at a time, knowing I'm the one preparing his meals, bathing and caring for him, building a bond with him as if he were my very own, and make me responsible for his life, but I am not invited to celebrate it?"

Samantha's scowl seemed to become even more enraged at the question as she screamed, "Wrong!"

She pointed towards Timothy and added, "I make him responsible for his life, and you, you're just THE HELP!

Motherless Child

$\mathcal{K}$ira graduating from high school brought joy to her father. Kira was raised as an only child without her mother. Kira's father, Darion, takes care of her. Kira has never met her mother, Selena, but Darion gave her a picture of her mother when she was five years old. Not knowing her mother was painful for Kira. Every Mother's Day, she would pull out the picture of Selena just to look at it and wonder what could have been. Darion explained to Kira that her mother Selena didn't want to raise a child with someone she didn't love.

Darion graduated from Texas Southern University, so TSU was the first and final choice for Kira. When Kira entered into her dorm room, she immediately hit it off with her roommate, Dominique.

Kira was an only child, so being selfish came natural to her; this was the first time she had ever stayed in the same room with another person away from home. Surprisingly, she was okay with sharing all of her belongings with her new roommate.

Kira continued to get to know her new roommate Dominique, who she viewed as a sister. The two of them talked about everything and even helped each other with homework assignments.

One day, Dominique's brother, Darrell, came to visit to let Dominique know their mother was sick. Without any hesitation, Dominique rushed home to be by her mother's side. Kira could not relate or understand from the daughter-to-mother perspective. Dominique confided in Kira that her mother had sickle cell. Kira also suffered from sickle cell, and Darion would always rush her to the hospital, never leaving her side.

Kira really missed Dominique for those few days that she went to care for her mother. When Dominique returned, Kira was so ecstatic. Dominique returned with good news about her mother and it was great to see Dominique in good spirits.

One day, as Kira was sitting on her bed, she reflected on how lucky Dominique was to have a brother who would drive all the way from Oklahoma to pick her up and take her to see her mother.

A father, mother, and a brother surrounded Dominique. Kira was a bit envious, but she really loved Dominique and wished she had her life.

Thanksgiving was coming up, and Kira asked Dominique if she would come and spend Thanksgiving with her and Darion. Dominique wanted to, but said she couldn't because it was a family tradition to honor her grandmother on her mother's side; she couldn't miss it.

Dominique asked Kira if she wanted to come with her family instead. Of course, Kira picked up the phone and immediately called her father Darion to ask if it was okay.

"You can go, but you have to fly and see me the last two days of Thanksgiving weekend," said Darion. Kira packed her clothes so fast; Dominique had to tell her to slow down.

When Kira arrived, it was her first time ever seeing a home with so many bedrooms and that much green grass everywhere. As Dominique walked into the home, she saw so many people in one place that it scared her a little bit, yet the moment was beautiful. After meeting everyone, the last person to greet her was Dominique's mother.

Kira was so excited when she saw Dominique's mother walking towards her, but the tunnel vision of her presence was surreal.

Dominique's mother reached her hand out and began to speak, "So you are Kira. I have heard so much about you. I am her mother and my name is Selena."

Kira shook her hand and eventually asked if she could take a picture of her and Dominique.

After she took the picture, she went to the bathroom and sent the picture to her father Darion. Then she immediately called him on the phone; he answered quickly, and she told her father to look at the picture she sent. Darion did so.

"This is your mother! Where are you?" Darion asked.

"With Dominique. Selena is her mother, daddy," said Kira.

"Oh no, my dear! Are you okay?" asked Darion.

"I am okay, but I can't stop crying daddy

because when I met Dominique, I felt like I knew her my entire life, and she was placed in my life for a reason. I gotta go daddy," said Kira, and immediately hung up the phone.

Kira walked back into the living room and sat on the couch. She endured the pain of sitting at the same table with her mother and stayed silent.

"Why are you silent? Is everything okay?" asked Dominique.

"I'm fine. I am just ready to go home and see my father and my grandmother," said Kira.

"What's your people's last name?" Selena asked across the table.

"I don't think the last name matters, but my father's name is Darion, and I was told my mother's name was Selena. Does that ring a bell?" Kira responded sarcastically.

Selena quickly left the table and went into her bedroom, locking the door behind her. Everyone, including Selena's husband, didn't understand what was going on.

"I will get a hotel for the night and head back to Houston. I don't want to disrupt my mother's comfort zone," said Kira. As Kira was walking out the door, Dominique ran after her grabbing her arm.

"What are you talking about?" asked Dominique.

"Selena is my mother! The mother that didn't want me! She's the mother that I never knew! I have been carrying around this picture my whole life!" Kira rebutted with tears in her eyes, flashing the picture to Dominique.

Dominique grabbed Kira and begged her not to leave.

"If you leave, then I will never get to know my sister," said Dominique with love in her eyes.

"Having a sister was always my dream wish as a child. Please don't stop what God placed in front of the both of us," she continued.

"I will stay," said Kira.

Before Dominique could get her next sentence out, Selena ran towards her and got on her knees to beg for forgiveness.

"Please forgive me Kira, please, I beg you," asked Selena.

As Kira stood there, full of many emotions, she didn't quite know how to reply. The pain was almost too much to bear. Her whole life she had wondered about her mother. She wondered why her mother didn't want her. How could she leave her and never look back?

How Selfish...

***

Daddy,
How could she
let him steal my
innocence?

***

She Let Him Touch Me

$\mathscr{M}$eet Dasia. Picture a young girl, age seven, with a complexion of vanilla-cocoa-swirl bronze. She had hair that held soft loose curls which fell slightly below her shoulders. Her eyes were hazel green, she had dimples that could melt the coldest of hearts, and she held a quiet yet respectful demeanor.

She loved to play with her dollies. She would pile all her dollies on the bed and pretend that she was a teacher while writing on the chalkboard placed on her wall. She was a happy little girl.

Dasia was the only daughter of six siblings. Although she had five brothers, her mother gave birth to her much later in life than her brothers. She was 12 years younger than her mother's fifth son. Apparently, her mother never gave up on trying to have that girl.

By the time Dasia was 5, all but one of her brothers had already moved out of the home. They had either gone off to college or moved into their own place. Dasia didn't have the same father as her brothers. Dasia's father and mother never married or resulted in a long-term relationship. They had big plans, but shortly after Dasia was born, her parents separated. Her father was off raising a new family. She hadn't seen her father since she was four, but she would hear her mom talk about him on the phone to her friends.

Although Dasia was not living with both her mother and father, she did have a step-dad. Silvia, Dasia's mother, had let Mr.B move in when Dasia was 5. He would spoil her. Every day he would come home with some sort of sweets: skittles, soda, hot Cheetos, you name it.

Mr. B was much older than Silvia, but he was mild mannered, well groomed, suave, and successful. He owned his own accounting firm and did all of the book-keeping for the celebrities.

Having Mr. B around exposed Dasia and her mother to a life that a princess would appreciate. But after a while, Silvia wasn't as attracted to Mr. B and would no longer give in to his late night advances towards her.

It wasn't long before Mr. B made sweet little Dasia his new project. It started with him pretending to let her drive the big truck while sitting in his lap as he drove around the neighborhood school parking lot. Dasia loved to sit on Mr. B's lap. She never got a chance to know her real father, but Mr. B was as close to having a father as Dasia could get. Mr. B would grab her by her crotch whenever she would move on or off his lap. Dasia would ask him not to grab her so tight and he would apologize, so whatever worry little Dasia felt at the moment would vanish when her step dad apologized with so much care in his eyes.

Silvia became so preoccupied with her freedom and the ability to travel without being tied down to 6 children that she didn't even notice the change in Mr. B's behavior or the fact that Dasia was spending more and more time locked away in her room.

Mr. B had started fondling Dasia on a regular basis. He would call them "love touches". Whenever he would want to touch her, he would make sure to have her treats in hand. He had convinced little Dasia that if she told anyone, she would get in a world of trouble, and her Mommy would be mad at her. Her little impressionable mind believed him.

One day, Mr. B decided to be bold. It was approximately 2:33 PM on a Saturday afternoon. Silvia had come in early that morning on a flight from Vegas, so she was sound asleep from not resting in the last 36 hours. Dasia's brother had gone with his older brothers for the weekend, and Dasia sat on the living room couch combing the hair of her cabbage patch doll.

Mr. B sat next to Dasia on the couch and covered her mouth. As he covered her mouth with one hand, he pushed her down on the couch with the other. Just as he was pulling her panties down her ankles, Silvia walked in the room.

"Mommie!" called out Dasia as she watched her mother quickly turn to go back to her room.

Mr.B was caught red handed, but what did it mean? As Mr. B jumped up to compose himself, he knew he could not chase Silvia with a full-on erection. He turned away from Dasia and she made a run for it. She ran after her mother, confused about what was happening. But when she reached her mother's room, her mother had locked the door.

"Go to your room!" yelled Silvia from the other side of the door. Dasia stood there. She was confused and crying, unsure of what all of that meant.

100

Thoughts consumed Dasia's mind. Why was Mr. B touching her? Was he right? Is she mad at me because she knows that Mr. B has been giving me love touches like he said?

As Dasia lay in her bed with a face full of tears, Mr. B entered her room and kneeled on the side of her bed. He reminded her not to tell a soul and reassured her that if she told her mother that nothing happened that her mother would love her again. And so she did.

The next day, Silvia and Mr. B behaved as if nothing had happened. Silvia did not seem to be bothered by what she saw the day before, but Dasia wasn't so sure, so she stuck to the script and remembered to always say "nothing happened".

Two weeks later when Silvia approached her about that day on the couch with Mr. B, Dasia looked down at her feet and mumbled, "Nothing happened."

Silvia grabbed Dasia in her arms and began to kiss and hug her. It seemed like Mr. B was right, as long as she said, "nothing happened", her mother loved her again.

Dasia is now an adult, and before she could get a resolution to this, Mr. B died. She always wondered if the lifestyle that Mr. B provided was the reason her mother chose to turn a blind eye to what happened on that couch that day and what continued to happen throughout her adolescent years. Dasia still doesn't have an answer to that question.

Dear Mama...

Dear Mama I

𝒟ear Mama,

You may not remember me since you left me in an alley. My birth name that you gave was Melissa, but my new name is Jasmine Drexler. I want to thank you for allowing me to travel from foster home to foster home. My first foster parents, The Jones, were really sweet, but the both of them would go out as a couple, leaving me with their son Joseph, and I hated it. At the age of 4, I never knew what my body parts were capable of or what a boy's body part could do for that matter.

When the social worker would come and visit, she would ask me if anyone was bothering me or if I was being touched inappropriately. As a child, I wondered what the word inappropriate meant, so I asked the social worker to explain. When she did, I kindly expressed to her that I didn't know it was inappropriate since Joseph told me not to tell anyone.

The Joneses were kind parents, but since Joseph was touching me in areas he shouldn't have been, I was moved to live with the Griffin family. I learned so much from them, especially the definition of racism and what color my skin was. Living in their basement for one month and only being allowed to eat once each day really made me wonder and think about what you looked like.

While my stomach was filled with hunger pains, I would often dream of the color of your skin, and wonder if you looked like Mrs. Griffin or if you resembled Mrs. Jones. My dreams would get interrupted when the bowl of oatmeal was thrown down the stairs, and I would have to use my fingers to eat the small piles from the floor. I sometimes would get creative and try to catch them as if I was in the matrix.

One night as I was sleeping, the Griffin's daughter, Alicia, came down to the basement to bring me a glass of water and a sandwich. When Alice handed me the sandwich, I tore into it like I was opening a Christmas present on Christmas Eve.

Alicia told me they were going out of town for a week, and I would be left alone for four days with no food and water. She felt that was so wrong of her parents. Alicia left me the key and told me to run when the sun would beam brightly through the upper window.

When I felt the sun blinding my eyes, I walked up the stairs very slowly, placed the key into the door, and turned cautiously. I ran so fast out the front door. I stopped at the end of the street and looked left then right; I decided to go right and not stop. When I arrived at a main street, I just walked and walked. Eventually, I walked into a store and asked for water.

Mr. Drexler, the storeowner, asked me where my parents were. I replied kindly by stating that my mama did not want me. Mr. Drexler looked at my body and was in disbelief of how skinny I was. Mr. Drexler was an old man around the age of 60.

Mr. Drexler left the store to his employees and took me to the hospital. Before we got to the hospital, Mr. Drexler took me to a nice restaurant. When we walked in, I was really shocked because I had never seen that many people so finely dressed. Mr. Drexler passed me crackers, and I ate almost 20 of them. When I looked up at Mr. Drexler, his eyes were filled with water as if he knew me since I was a baby. Mr. Drexler asked me what I wanted to eat, and since I couldn't read, I said, "Mr. Drexler, I don't know what's inside the papers."

"Well, this is an Italian restaurant, and this place is filled with noodle dishes," said Mr. Drexler. "Do you like spaghetti?" he continued.

"I've never had it," I replied. He ordered it for me and when it came, I looked at it and wondered if it was really mine. If it is, should I eat it now or save it for later? I thought to myself.

"Eat up baby girl," said Mr. Drexler. So I did. When we were finished, Mr. Drexler took my hand and walked me to the car. He even opened my car door. He drove me to the hospital and sat in the room with me. While we were waiting on the doctor and social worker, Mr. Drexler's wife came in. She reminded me of Diahann Carroll. She walked in like a celebrity. She came in and gave me a hug, saying it was going to be okay.

Mr. and Mrs. Drexler pulled the social worker to the side and spoke with her before she could speak with me. Of course, I couldn't hear what they were saying. My body was so tired that I fell straight to sleep. I slept for 12 hours. When I woke up the next day, Mrs. Drexler was standing right in front of me, smiling.

"I brought you some clothes and toys to play

with," said Mrs. Drexler.

"All of these are for me?" I asked.

"Of course, darling," said Mrs. Drexler.

At that moment, I realized the Drexlers were either kind or rich. As I was lying there, Mrs. Drexler spoke with the social worker and then turned to me, "So are you ready to move to your new spot?"

"New spot, what do you mean?" I asked.

"I am retired. Mr. Drexler owns the store you ran into. Our two oldest boys are gone. We have this huge 7-bedroom house with no one to share it with, and we would love for you to live with us until the adoption is final," said Mrs. Drexler.

"So I will stay with you and Mr. Drexler until I move to another home?" I asked.

"You can stay with us as long as you like. We are about to finalize the adoption of you, sweet baby," said Mrs. Drexler.

At that moment Mom, I felt important and special. Running from that home led me to the Drexler's. Mom, I am now 20 years old. I want to again thank you for not wanting me. I want you to know I forgive you, and I love you.

Finally free,
Me

Covered Lies

Daughter: Mommy, he hurt me.

Mother: Who?

Daughter: Jeffrey touched me and it hurt.

Mother: Stop lying. You know my husband would not do that. Don't ever say that again!!

Dear Mama II

*D*ear Mama,

Hey Mama, you see me, but you don't see me. You are probably asking yourself what does that mean. I would see you at family gatherings and various family functions, and every time I would see you, I figured you were a cousin or a distant relative. Walking into the house with my Uncle Neo hand and hand, he would always stop me on the porch and say, "Baby girl, you are beautiful, you are so special and anything that comes your way just know that you are destined for success."

At the time Mama, I didn't know what he meant. Sitting on the couch in Big Mama's house, I would look around at everyone. I would just sit there waiting for my family to come and kiss me on the cheek. I noticed at all family functions; a particular woman sitting at the dinner table would never come up to me. As a little girl, I figured that the woman just liked to be alone. When it was time to hold hands and pray before Thanksgiving dinner, I would walk up to that same lady just to see if she would move around again to avoid holding my hand in prayer.

The child in me wanted to approach her, rub her hair, and embrace her face with my hands. This fantasy would come to mind every holiday and family celebration. As I got older and walked past the lady from the table, I started to see my reflection in her. We even had the same facial features; not to mention, she even walked like me.

108

Mama, I just want you to know I have always known you were that woman sitting at the table, refusing to hold my hand during family prayer. Whatever the reasons you chose not to keep me, take care of me, or acknowledge me, I just want you to know it would have been nice of you to say what everyone else in the family said to me, "Hello, it is good to see you and I love you."

Love you,
Nikki

Dear Mama III

Dear Mama,

When I realized you were my mother and not the aunt who raised me, my heart was filled with joy. I can't blame you for not wanting to keep me since I was conceived at the age of 14. As your son, I have a few questions. When you became of age, why did you take a job that would keep you away from me? When you were able to spend one-on-one time with me, why did you choose to go out on dates with various men? Why Mama? When I was a little boy, you would call me and tell me the weekend coming up was our time. I would have my bag packed, ready to go, and you would not show up. Why Mama?

When you met your husband, he didn't want to be bothered with me; I was told to stay at my aunt's house. Why would you allow him to do this when I don't know my biological father?

Now that I have a child, Mama, the pattern is happening again. I didn't realize that being selfish can actually be passed down from mother to son. Mama, you asked me why I treat women wrong and show no respect for them. I believe the reason for this is you. Hopefully, you can take time out of your busy schedule to sit down with me and answer these questions...

Best Regards,
Daniel

Please Come Get Me Daddy

Daughter: Mama, since Mr. Michael is sending you to Vegas for the weekend can I go with my daddy.

Mother: Until he pays that child support, you can't go over there.

Daughter: But please mama, just this one time. Please! I don't like staying here with him.

Mr. Michael: With who?

Mother: She doesn't want to stay, because she wants to go to her dad's this weekend.

Mr. Michael: No. Leave her here. I don't want to deal with your baby daddy while you're out of town. I'll take care of her. She will be just fine.

Daughter runs to call father on the phone in the other room. The phone rings but the voicemail picks up.

Daughter: Daddy, please pick up. I need you to come get me. She's leaving me here with Mr. Michael again. Please don't let her leave me here alone with him...

Dear Mama IV

$\mathcal{D}$ear Mama,

I hope this letter finds you, and I hope you are doing well. The story I heard, is that my father Sorrell and you had a great relationship, but then Sorrell started seeing some changes in you. Sorrell found crack pipes under the bed, and you would be gone for days at a time. I woke up one morning in the arms of my grandmother and grandfather. Of course, I don't remember all the details because I was only 3 years old.

As I would walk the halls and hear my aunt Sonya and my dad call grandmother Mama, I started to believe my grandmother was my Mama. Getting older, I realized that the woman I had been calling Mama, was really my grandmother. As a troubled child, I didn't realize that you were on drugs and decided to pursue prostitution as a lifestyle.

I made a point in my life not to fall in your footsteps. Every time I would ask my father about meeting you, he would kindly tell me it was not the right time. My great aunt Vivian worked for the police department, so she came to the house because she heard I was so eager to meet my biological mother.

Aunt Vivian gave me a file, and when I opened it, there were pictures of you. Mugshot after mugshot after mugshot. As I continued to look through the papers, the file revealed I had a total of eight brothers and sisters all in the system. The pages brought tears to my eyes. When I read you were a thief, heavy drug user, have multiple felonies on your record, and been a prostitute, my heart sank. This is not the fantasy I imagined every day when I saw mothers and daughters holding hands while walking in the store or in school.

So Mama, please understand that I am writing you this letter, hoping that you will have a kind heart towards me, and take the time to see me so I can sit down with you to get your side of the story. Please let me know if this is possible.

Good day,
Shawn

Happy
Mother's Day
to all the
Fathers doing
it themselves...

You're upset with me
as your daughter, for
praising
my father's wife
on Mother's Day,
but I only hear from
you on Mother's Day?

Counsel Sessions I:

Therapist: What is going on with your son?

BD: My son is becoming more and more stubborn these days.

Therapist: Do you have any idea why?

BD: When I spoke with him, he said he doesn't want to talk about it. Being that I am his father, I have a problem with him brushing me off. What really upsets me is he is becoming very standoffish towards me.

Therapist: Do you think it has something to do with him not seeing his mother in years?

BD: It could be, but he needs to man up and let it go.

Therapist: Easier said than done.

BD: My mother wasn't around, and I sucked it up and moved on.

Therapist: Well, have you given any thought that he won't speak with you because you will just compare your story to his by making your excuse and your way of solving the problem the only solution? I think you should take him to dinner and speak about how you felt when your mother wasn't there. Share the methods you used to become strong and how you didn't allow her absence to interfere with your progress. Wait for him to respond. This should open up a dialogue between you two, and he may open up about his feelings to you.

BD: I will try that.

Did you forget about

ME

for Mother's Day since

YOU

are playing Mama to someone
else's

KIDS?

Boyfriend Saga I

BM: My boyfriend and I want to take Drake to the theatre this weekend. I know this is your scheduled weekend to be with Drake, but I really want Drake to bond with my boyfriend Oscar.

BD: You know I purchased tickets to go to the theatre, and I spoke with you about picking him up Thursday night instead of Friday for the weekend.

BM: I know, but can you please just do this for me? I am tired of being single, and Oscar made it clear he wanted to start bonding with Drake.

BD: Let me speak with Drake please.

BM: Ok, let me go get him. Hold please.

(Baby mama walks to bedroom to get Drake to come to the phone.)

Drake: Hey daddy, what's going on?

BD: I'm good. Would you rather go to the movies this weekend with Oscar or me?

Drake: *(holds the phone in silence; someone is speaking to him softly in the background.)*

BD: Drake, you there?

Drake: Yes.

BD: You want to go with me?

Drake: Yes.

(Oscar snatches the phone.)

Oscar: Look here, we are working on being a family, so Drake doesn't have a say-so on this. He needs a father every day, not every other weekend.

BD: Dude, please give the phone back to MY son so WE can have a discussion on what HE wants to do this weekend.

(Oscar hangs up phone.)

Some baby mamas want companionship so bad they would place the child's father in a situation to not be a father.

How selfish...

YOU

want me to acknowledge

YOU

for Mother's Day but

YOU

only are my Mommy when it is
convenient for

YOU?

A Plot for Pay

$\mathcal{A}$s a father, Dennis realized not being in the home was the best decision for him and Allison in order to move forward in a positive manner. Dennis received weekly calls from Allison with her multiple requests. Listening to her continuously ask was on the annoying scale, but realizing a father's role, Dennis accepted it all. When Dennis received the request to purchase his son Derrick a cell phone and desktop computer, Dennis immediately went on a lunch break to pick it up for Derrick.

When the clock struck 5:00p.m., and Dennis clocked out from work, he went straight to Allison's home to drop off the merchandise. When Dennis arrived to Allison's home, Derrick was nowhere to be found. This truly disappointed Dennis as a father. Not being able to see the smile on his son's face or see his eyes light up like high beams when receiving the gift was rather disappointing to him. He took so much joy in seeing Derrick smile.

"Where is Derrick?" Dennis asked.

"He is over his friend's home doing homework," Allison replied.

As a father who had been in Derrick's shoes, he didn't want to interrupt him with his peers to cause a certain level of embarrassment. Dennis realized his weekend was in a few days, and he could discuss it with Derrick then.

Allison decided to drop Derrick off for the upcoming visitation weekend, which felt a bit strange to Dennis. Instead of questioning and being petty, Dennis decided to dismiss the idea of an unnecessary argument.

While Dennis and Derrick were enjoying father and son time, Dennis asked Derrick about his cell phone.

"So son, how does having your own cell phone make you feel?" asked Dennis.

"Seeing all my friends with their cell phones made me so jealous and envious, but when I saw the cell phone on the bed, I jumped for joy and was truly happy inside," Derrick replied.

Seeing the smile on Derrick's face made Dennis almost tear up. He had to remember he was a man and didn't want his son to see him cry, especially over a cell phone. He let Derrick know how excited he was to drop off the phone earlier in the week, but wished he could have given it to him personally.

"Dad, I didn't know you bought the phone for me," said Derrick.

Dennis paused, kept a level head, and said, "Yes, I did son, your mother called me that morning, and I rushed right to the store during my lunch break to pick it up."

The look on Derrick's face appeared confusing. Dennis reassured Derrick that the importance of who purchased it was not relevant.

"I know you love your phone, but how is the desktop computer working for you?" asked Dennis.

Complete silence filled the room, and Derrick slowly responded, "What desktop computer?"

Dennis figured his son didn't know what the word "desktop" meant, so he said, "Boy stop playing with me...the computer I dropped off with the phone."

Derrick looked at his father with a sad face and confused expression, "Daddy, I didn't receive a computer. Are you sure you dropped it off?"

Dennis, being the calm and levelheaded father, expressed a state of confusion by saying, "Maybe I am confused, disregard it son."

Dennis decided to drop Derrick off early in hopes of catching Allison off guard and speak with her about the computer. When Dennis arrived, Allison wasn't there. Allison's older daughter, Arissa, answered the door. Dennis gave her a hug and asked her if she enjoyed using the new computer he dropped off a few days prior.

"Mom sold the computer to pay the mortgage. She was two months behind," said Arissa. Dennis wanted to destroy all the furniture in the home and punch a few holes in the wall, but instead he replied, "I didn't know Allison was behind on the mortgage, do you mind if I sit and wait for her?" asked Dennis.

"No problem, I'm headed out to meet my fiancé for dinner," said Arissa.

The longer Dennis sat there, his head started to ache, and his body felt numb. Right at the height of ugliness, Allison walked in the door.

"Hey Dennis," said Allison.

Dennis looked at her, wanting to take his hands and place them around her neck, but instead he took a deep breath and calmly asked, "Where is the computer you sold?"

"Huh, who told you that?" asked Allison. At that moment, so much silence filled the room that a pin drop could be heard four streets over. Dennis just paused and looked into Allison's eyes. Since Allison was married to Dennis before, she knew exactly what look that was and immediately began to cry.

She ran up to Dennis hoping to wrap her arms around him for some type of "moral" support, but instead Dennis pushed her away, reminding her of the $1,500.00 he paid in child support and the long list of items he would purchase for Derrick and Arissa.

124

As a father, Dennis believed she really needed the money, but he also felt it was unnecessary to lie. From that day on, he promised to never drop off items directly to Allison; he would give the items directly to Derrick.

Boyfriend Saga II

BD: *(knocks on the door)*

Boyfriend: Hey, what's up?

BD: Who are you?

Boyfriend: Why?

BD: I am here to pick up my daughter. Is her mother here?

Boyfriend: No, she had something to do, but she is in her room. Let me get her.

BD: Do you live here?

Boyfriend: Sometimes.

BD: *(takes his daughter hand in hand)*

So, as a baby mama, you would not call the father to tell him of a man living in the home? And this man is babysitting as well?

How selfish...

More Money More Lies

$\mathscr{B}$aby mamas living off welfare and taking the government for all it can give is a frustration many baby daddies complain about. Some baby daddies pay over $1,000.00 per month in child support to single mothers who are getting food stamps, government checks, and housing.

The baby daddies are not complaining about the free services; they are complaining about baby mamas staying at home and not trying to get a job. Since the internet is in most homes, and home-based businesses are growing, many baby daddies have a problem with the message, "I don't have time to work; I have to take care of all my kids."

Peter's baby mama has six kids from six different men. Peter accepts the blame in getting Sasha pregnant, but says he didn't know she had six kids from six different men at the time. The oldest three were gone and living their life as adults. Peter is Daddy #6, and he pays close to $800.00 in child support.

Sasha, Peter's baby mama, gets food stamps and a check for the other two children in the home, Monica and Monique. Peter, being a good dude, realized she was receiving government assistance because the fathers of the other two kids were not paying child support. When Sasha told Peter they were having a baby, Peter was very excited to add another boy to the family. Without hesitation, Sasha named their son Peter Jr.

As the two of them tried to make it work, he began finding out so many secrets Sasha was holding. The first secret was her three older kids. While he was at the home assisting Sasha with their son, the three oldest kids, Jeremiah, Zion, and Morris, walked in. Sasha had never told Peter about them. But they introduced themselves as her children.

His mouth dropped. He knew she had two, but knowing she had a total of five and from five different men really scared him. All four of them sat down on the couch and started conversing. Jeremiah mentioned running into Monica's father, who gave Jeremiah a check during their encounter.

"That's nice of him to finally give Sasha money for Monica," said Peter.

"Yeah, he is a good dude. My mom didn't even have to file child support on him, so he is not in the system with the Attorney General's office. He just gives my mom a check every month," said Jeremiah.

Peter was boiling inside. He remembered having a conversation with Sasha when she told him he needed to pay $800.00 per month because she needed the extra money to take care of her other

128

two kids. When Peter saw the amount of the check was $1,500.00, he wanted to fall to the floor and start kicking like a child throwing a tantrum.

"He just started paying child support?" asked Peter.

"He works out of town, so he doesn't see my sister often. To make up for it, he started paying child support in the amount of $1,500.00 almost 10 years ago," explained Jeremiah.

Peter didn't want the kids to know how angry he was, so he continued to laugh and joke with them. When Sasha came home, the older kids were playing with the younger kids. The check was on the coffee table.

"Sasha, here, Jeremiah brought this for you," said Peter. Peter handed the check to her, and she placed it in her purse.

"You wanna explain to me that check you happen to receive every month?" asked Peter.

"What are you talking about? He decided just yesterday he wanted to pay child support," said Sasha.

"Jeremiah, come here please," called Peter.

"Hey, Monica's dad is a good father for paying child support every month. You think so, Jeremiah?" asked Peter.

"He sure is. Better than my own father and the amount he gives every month shows he really cares for her," replied Jeremiah.

Peter aggressively expressed, "Sasha, I will ask you again to explain that check to me, and why you lied to me about not receiving child support from Monica's dad."

Peter is still waiting on an answer from Sasha...

*

***

If you are a mother every other weekend, does this make you a single mother?

***

*

Lazy Mom

My son, Sam, was a phenomenal kid in school. His mother worked a part-time job, and I made sure neither one of them had to want for anything. My baby mama Daloris was never the "wifey type". She even refused to cook or clean.

During our marriage, I had to do all of the cooking and cleaning. When we decided to part ways, being able to see my son was not a problem that arose between Daloris and I.

Since cooking wasn't really her thing, my son ate hamburgers, fries, pizza, and tacos almost every day. When Sam would come and visit me, I made sure to cook him a home-cooked meal with lots of vegetables. He hated it, but he knew he could not get up from the table until he ate all of it.

By the time my son started attending high school, he didn't come over as much because he was a football and basketball player. Between the practices and games, it seemed that he rarely had any weekends that he was not scheduled to practice or play.

Sam made the cut for the varsity basketball team and seemed to be excelling in the sport. In fact, he had done so well that there were several colleges already scouting for him.

His senior year had finally come, and it was the championship game. I was so proud to be there, watching my son make high school history. He was moving and shaking on them boys. The crowd was screaming in excitement, cheering him on.

I couldn't help but notice that he appeared to be a bit flushed in the face. I figured that it was the adrenaline running through his body that had him so winded. As he went to dunk on the opposing team, he scored, but Sam fell to the floor. His mother and I immediately ran to him.

When he arrived at the hospital, the doctor said, "Sam had a massive heart attack."

"Doctor, how can my son who is only 17 years old have a massive heart attack?" asked Daloris.

"His arteries were really clogged from not eating right. This could potentially be the reason that his blood pressure was at an all-time high," said the doctor.

After the doctor explained all the problems my son had, my concern seemed to grow in regards to his ability to participate in sports.

I asked the doctor when he could return to the court, and he replied, "Sam will never be able to play football or basketball again."

Knowing how much my son loved sports, I couldn't imagine having to break the news to him. The words that the doctor expressed hurt my heart and cut like a knife.

Wow, should I be mad at my baby mama for not taking better care of my son by ensuring that he had better eating habits?

Poetry for a Selfish Baby Mama

Praying

Every day I pray, you let me see my son...

I pray you let me pick him up from school a few days each week.

Every day I pray, you let me see my son...

I pray you let me come over sometimes to help my son with his homework.

Every day I pray, you let me see my son...

I pray you let my mother see my son on a weekly basis.

Every day I pray, you let me see my son...

I pray that you call me so I can participate in school functions.

Every day I pray, you let me see my son...

I pray you let him call me and say goodnight.

Every day I pray, you let me see my son...

I pray you let my son honor me on Father's Day.

Every day I pray, you let me see my son...

I pray you just find it in your heart to open the door when I ring the doorbell.

Please let me be a father to my son...

I know she is his mother, but Heavenly Father, can you please help me? All I want to do is be a father to my son...

-Ablyss

It's You

I want to be there
I want to help you everyday

There is no peace with you
Arguing daily is not healthy for you
It's not healthy for me

When I call to come through
You have excuses that are not true

Now my son thinks I don't love him
I don't want to see him

But if he knew the truth
He would know
It's not me
It's you

It's not me
It's you

-Ablyss

Never Good Enough

The word Priority.......
What does that mean to you?
I no longer own a house
I no longer drive a fancy car
done with shopping for myself
my vegan diet is gone
it's all about the bootleg

Doesn't matter what I do, it's never good enough for
you...

What does that mean to you?

I pay you child support
place cash in your hands
repair your vehicle
bring you'll groceries

you still limit my time with our little girl...

doesn't matter what I do
it's never good enough for you

father and daughter time is unimportant to you
precious moments are insignificant to you
ignoring my phone calls is petty of you

you continuously make me feel irrelevant

doesn't matter what I do
it's never good enough for you

-Ablyss

A Father's Right

I am a man. All man.
I am a father. A real father.
I am a Dad. A real Dad.

On Mondays, I come by just to play basketball with
him.

On Tuesdays, I fall through to cook for the two of
you because I love him.

I want to spend all of my free time with him.

On Wednesdays, I come by to mow the lawn.
I want to teach him.

On Thursdays, I go to work late so I can take our son
to school because I love him.

On Fridays, I leave work early and rush to your
home to pick up our son because I adore him.

Please don't ever stop letting me be a father to my
son.

I am a man. All man.
I am a father. A real father.
I am a Dad. A real Dad.

-Ablyss

Revenge

She didn't care that he needed money to live.
She found it hard to forgive.

She felt mistreated
Because he cheated

She sacrificed so much to make it work
She only ended up hurt

She's on a mission to get revenge
Her only weapon is his money and his kids...

-Onney

Scandalous

We poking holes now?

Your manipulative mind
persuaded me to lay down with you

I didn't provide protection
since you had it for us two

So we poking holes now
we setting traps now
popping pills in the drink now
making me dizzy now

seducement
the plot of evil
inveiglement

you are just evil
you do this all
since I placed you back in the friend zone
since we not on that level

hook the snag

I overheard your conversation
with your friends
and again I ask you

WE POKING HOLES NOW?

-Ablyss

Reflection
"The Liberation of a Lil' Brown Girl"

I'm on the verge of a break up.
A break up to make up all of the inconsistencies that
I have found within me...
So yes, I am breaking up with myself!
It's not about anyone else,
because when it's all said and done and the trouble
hits the fan,
I am the only one left to take the stand,
and I understand what bad choices can do.
Bad choices can make you look like the fool,
bad choices can make you seem so uncouth –
I tell you the truth that, I HAVE HAD MY SHARE!!

So as I stand in the mirror, I can't stand to see
the reflection staring back at me.
So it's time that I remove all of the trash and debris,
plus the makeup!
And take up some advice from my old friend Seven...
like he said, "it's not about Mary Kay, Fashion Fair or
Mac; it's the personal baggage that's attached,"
and I refuse to be the bag lady!
So today I am breaking up with me!
Because when I look in that mirror, I can't stand the
reflection that I see.

Now don't get me wrong.
Everything I see is not bad,
but it's sad, because as I look beyond the surface of
the reflection and look into my own eyes,

the pain I have inflicted on myself
makes me want to cry.

How can I make bad decisions in relationships
and then have the audacity
to turn around and ask God, why me?
How can I love a man more than I love myself?
How can I put everything else before my well-being
and put my priorities on a shelf?
It's time to wake up, so I am going to shake up
myself with a personal break up
so I can be a better me
and be satisfied with the reflection I see
in that mirror staring back at me.

Yes I am a great mother to my sons
and I love all three, yes indeed.
But where's the man that planted those seeds?
The problem was I put his wants before my needs!
The problem was I never had time to BREATHE,
a mother at the young age of 16!
Yeah I may have finished school
but I have disillusioned myself with love
by playing the fool...
Not just once, but twice
so I have to tell myself
that something just ain't right.

You can't do the same thing
expecting different results,
that mathematical equation will never add up.
The problem wasn't them, it was me
because I allowed those men to treat me unfairly

My first husband beat on me
and my second husband cheated on me
and I stuck around way too long
because I didn't think that I was worthy.
That mindset was embedded in my mentality
leaving me to be
a product of my environment on the inside,
so I wore a smile on the outside
trying to hide my dismay, but today I AM FREE!
I am free from your judgment of me,
I am free to be whomever I want to be,
even if you don't find it satisfactory.

I am breaking up with me because I will no longer be
- bound by the molestation that happened to me
from the dead man I had to call step-daddy,
I will no longer be bound
by extension cord beatings
and mother screaming
YOU B****! YOU AINT GONE BE S***!

I owe it to that little black girl
who was lost in this dark world
a new beginning with a happy ending.
SHE DESERVES TO BE FINALLY BE HAPPY.
She deserves a life that's tear free
and full of possibilities.

 All my life I have lived just to prove them wrong!
I've written books, songs, and recited poems,
starred in stage plays
and executive produced my own CD,
even did a few movies,

But still I couldn't seem to break away
from the shackles that held me
because with all that success I still felt empty.
I still thought that it was my image
that would make me!

But I was sadly mistaken,
because they say imitation
is the best form of flattery,
but not when you're imitating being happy!
Not when your closest friends
turn out to be your enemies.

I would walk through the poetry lounge
with this great big smile,
making sure my hair was on point
and my clothes were in style.
But who the hell cares?
I wasn't content
even when I did get compliments.

This was my get away
from the reality of dealing with ME,
and so...we're breaking up!
All those things I went through
I never let go and forgot...
I am making up my mind to say
that isn't what LIFE'S about!

I want to be free...
so I am breaking up with me,
because when I look in the mirror
do you know who I need to see?

I need to see a God-fearing,
faith-having,
bold,
beautiful
and secure black woman
staring back at me!

And that is what I call
A REFLECTION of Perfection...

What Is Child Support?

In family law and public policy, **child support** (or **child maintenance**) is an ongoing, periodic payment made by a parent for the financial benefit of a child following the end of a marriage or other relationship. Child maintenance is paid directly or indirectly by an *obligor* to an *obligee* for the care and support of children of a relationship that has been terminated, or in some cases never existed. Often the obligor is a non-custodial parent. The obligee is typically a custodial parent, a caregiver, a guardian, or the state.

Depending on the jurisdiction, a custodial parent may pay child support to a non-custodial parent. Typically, one has the same duty to pay child support irrespective of sex, so a mother is required to pay support to a father just as a father must pay a mother. In some jurisdictions where there is joint custody, the child is considered to have two custodial parents and no non-custodial parents, and a custodial parent with a higher income (obligor) may be required to pay the other custodial parent (obligee). In other jurisdictions even with legally shared residence, unless they can prove exactly equal contributions, one parent will be deemed the non-resident parent for child support and will have to pay the other parent a proportion of their income, the "resident" parent's income or needs are not assessed.

In family law, child support is often arranged as part of a divorce, martial separation, annulment, determination of parentage or dissolution of a civil union and may supplement alimony (spousal support) arrangements. The right to child support and the responsibilities of parents to provide such support have been internationally recognized. The 1992 United Nations Convention on the Rights of the Child is a binding convention signed by every member nation of the United Nations and formally ratified by all but South Sudan and the United States. It declares that the upbringing and development of children and a standard of living adequate for the children's development is a common responsibility of both parents and a fundamental human right for children, and asserts that the primary responsibility to provide such for the children rests with their parents. Other United Nations documents and decisions related to child support enforcement include the 1956 New York Convention on the Recovery Abroad of Maintenance created under the auspices of the United Nations, which has been ratified by the 64 of the UN member state.

In addition, the right to child support, as well as specific implementation and enforcement measures, has been recognized by various other international entities, including the Council of

148

Europe, the European Union and the Hague Conference.

Within individual countries, examples of legislation pertaining to, and establishing guidelines for, the implementation and collection of child maintenance include the 1975 Family Law Act(Australia), the Child Support Act (United Kingdom) and the Maintenance and Affiliation Act (Fiji) Child support in the United States, 45 C.F.R. 302.56 requires each state to establish and publish a Guideline that is presumptively correct, and Review the Guideline, at a minimum, every four (4) years. Child support laws and obligations are known to be recognized in a vast majority of world nations, including the majority of countries in Europe, North America and Australasia, as well as many in Africa, Asia and South America.

Information Provided by Wikipedia
https://en.wikipedia.org/wiki/Child_support

Who Is the Attorney General?

In most common law jurisdictions, the **attorney general** or **attorney-general** is the main legal advisor to the government, and in some jurisdictions they may also have executive responsibility for law enforcement, prosecutions or even responsibility for legal affairs generally. In practice, the extent to which the attorney-general personally provides legal advice to the government varies between jurisdictions, and even between individual office-holders within the same jurisdiction, often depending on the level and nature of the office-holder's prior legal experience.

The term was originally used to refer to any person who holds a general power of attorney to represent a principal in all matters. In the common law tradition, anyone who represents the state, especially in criminal prosecutions, is such an attorney. Although a government may designate some official as the permanent attorney general, anyone who comes to represent the state in the same way may, in the past, be referred to as such, even if only for a particular case. Today, however, in most jurisdictions the term is largely reserved as a title of the permanently appointed attorney general of the state, sovereign or other member of the royal family. The term is pluralized attorneys general or attorneys-general.

Civil law jurisdictions have similar offices, who may be variously called "procurators", "advocates general", "public attorneys", and other titles. Many of these offices also use "attorney general" or "attorney-general" as the English translation of the title, although because of different historical provenance the nature of such offices is usually different from that of attorneys-general in common law jurisdictions.

In the federal government of the United States, the Attorney General is a member of the Cabinet and, as head of the Department of Justice, is the top law enforcement officer and lawyer for the government. The attorney general may need to be distinguished from the Solicitor General, a high Justice Department official with the responsibility of representing the government before the Supreme Court. In cases of exceptional importance, however, the Attorney General may choose personally to represent the government to the Supreme Court.

The individual U.S. states and territories, as well as the Federal capital of Washington, D.C., also have attorneys general with similar responsibilities. The majority of state Attorneys General are chosen by popular election, as opposed to the U.S. Attorney General, who is a presidential appointee confirmed by the Senate.

In nearly all United States jurisdictions the Attorney General is the chief law enforcement officer of that jurisdiction, and as such Attorney General may also be considered a police rank. The proper form of addressing a person holding the office of Attorney General is "Mister/Madam Attorney General," or "Attorney General," and referred to as "Attorney General." The shorthand form of address is "General." The plural is "Attorneys General" or "Attorneys-General". It is common in U.S. state governments that the state attorney general is addressed as "general." It is less commonplace that the federal attorney general is so addressed, though no less proper to do so.

Information Provided by Wikipedia
https://en.wikipedia.org/wiki/Attorney_general

Child Custody

Child custody and **legal-guardianship** are legal terms which are used to describe the legal and practical relationship between a parent and his or her child, such as the right of the child to make decisions and the parent's duty to care for the child.

Following ratification of the United Nations Convention on the Rights of the Child in most countries, terms such as "residence" and "contact" (known as "visitation" in the United States) have superseded the concepts of "custody" and "access". Instead of a parent having "custody" of or "access" to a child, a child is now said to "reside" or have "contact" with a parent. For a discussion of the new international nomenclature, see parental responsibility.

Residence and contact issues typically arise in proceedings involving divorce (dissolution of marriage), annulment, and other legal proceedings where children may be involved. In most jurisdictions the issue of which parent the child will reside with is determined in accordance with the best interests of the child standard.

Family law proceedings which involve issues of residence and contact often generate the most acrimonious disputes. While most parents cooperate when it comes to sharing their children and resort to mediation to settle a dispute, not all do. For those that engage in litigation, there seem to be few limits. Court filings quickly fill with mutual accusations by one parent against the other, including sexual, physical, and emotional abuse, brain-washing, parental alienation syndrome, sabotage, and manipulation. It is these infrequent yet difficult custody battles that become public via the media and sometimes distort the public's perceptions so that the issues appear more prevalent than they are and the court's response appear inadequate.

Forum shopping to gain advantage occurs both between nations and where laws and practices differ between areas within a nation, The Hague Convention seeks to avoid this, also in the United States of America, the Uniform Child Custody Jurisdiction and Enforcement Act was adopted by all 50 states, family law courts were forced to defer jurisdiction to the home state.

In some places, courts and legal professionals are beginning to use the term parenting schedule instead of custody and visitation. The new terminology eliminates the distinction between custodial and noncustodial parents, and also attempts to build upon the best interests of the children by crafting schedules that meet the developmental needs of the children. For example, younger children need shorter, more frequent time

154

with parents, whereas older children and teenagers may demand less frequent shifts yet longer blocks of time with each parent.

Forms of Custody

- Alternating custody is an arrangement whereby the child/children live for an extended period of time with one parent and an alternate amount of time with the other parent. While the child/children are with the parent, that parent retains sole authority and responsibility over the child/children. This type of arrangement is also referred to as Divided custody. [1]

- Shared custody[2] is an arrangement whereby the child/children live for an extended period of time with one parent, and then for a similar amount of time with the other parent. Opposite to alternating custody, both parents retain authority over the child/children.

- Bird's nest custody is an arrangement whereby the parents go back and forth from a residence in which the child/children reside, placing the burden of upheaval and movement on the parents rather than the child/children.

- Joint custody is an arrangement whereby both parents have legal custody and/or physical custody.

- Sole custody is an arrangement whereby only one parent has physical and legal custody of the child/children.

- Split custody is an arrangement whereby one parent has full-time custody over some children, and the other parent has full custody over the other children.

- Third-party custody is an arrangement whereby the children do not remain with either biological parent, and are placed under the custody of a third person.

Physical Custody

Physical custody involves the day-to-day care of a child and establishes where a child will live. A parent with physical custody has the right to have his/her child live with him/her.

If a child lives with both parents, each parent shares "joint physical custody", and each parent is said to be a "custodial parent". Thus, in joint physical custody, neither parent is said to be a "non-custodial parent."[4] In joint physical custody, actual lodging and care of the child is shared according to a court-ordered custody schedule (also known as a "parenting plan" or "parenting schedule") In many cases, the term "visitation" is no longer used in this context, but rather is reserved to sole custody orders. Terms of art such as "primary custodial parent" and "primary residence" have no legal meaning other than for determining tax status, and both parents are still said to be "custodial parents".[5]

In some states, "joint physical custody" creates a presumption of "equal shared parenting". However, in most states, joint physical custody only creates an obligation to provide each of the parents with "significant periods" of physical custody so as to assure the child of "frequent and continuing contact" with both parents. Courts have not clearly defined what "significant periods" and "frequent and continuous contact" mean, which requires parents to litigate to find out.

If a child lives with one parent, that parent has "sole physical custody" and is said to be the "custodial parent" whereas the other parent is said to be the "non-custodial parent", but may have visitation rights or "visitation" with his/her child.

Joint physical custody

Joint physical custody is a court order whereby custody of a child is awarded to both parties. In joint custody, both parents are *custodial parents* and neither parent is a non-custodial parent; in other words, the child has two custodial parents.

Many states recognize two forms of joint custody: joint physical custody, and joint legal custody. In joint legal custody, both parents share the ability to have access to educational, health, and other records, and have equal decision-making status where the welfare of the child is concerned.

In joint physical custody, which would include joint physical care, actual lodging and care of the child is shared according to a court-ordered custody schedule (also known as a *parenting plan* or *parenting schedule*). In many cases, the term *visitation* is no longer used in these circumstances, but rather is reserved to sole custody orders.[7] In some states joint physical custody creates a presumption of equal shared parenting, however in most states, joint physical custody creates an obligation to provide each of the parents with "significant periods" of physical custody so as to assure the child of "frequent and continuing contact" with both parents. For example, states such as Alabama, California, and Texas do not necessarily require joint custody orders to result in substantially equal parenting time, whereas states such as Arizona, Georgia, and Louisiana do require joint custody orders to result in substantially equal parenting time where feasible. Courts have not clearly defined what "significant periods" and "frequent and continuous contact" mean, which requires parents to litigate to find out.

It is important to note that joint physical custody and joint legal custody are different aspects of custody, and determination is often made separately in many states' divorce courts. E.g., it is possible to have joint legal custody, but for one parent to have sole physical custody In some states this is referred to as Custodial Parent and Non-Custodial Parent.

Also, where there is joint physical custody, terms of art such as "primary custodial parent" and "primary residence" have no legal meaning other than for determining tax status, and both parents are still custodial parents.

Sole physical custody

Sole physical custody means that a child shall reside with and be under the supervision of one parent, subject to the power of the court to order visitation. Physical custody involves the day-to-day care of a child and establishes where a child will live. A parent with physical custody has the right to have his/her child live with him/her. If a child lives with only one parent, that parent has *sole physical custody* and is said to be the *custodial parent*. The other parent is said to be the *non-custodial parent*, and may have visitation rights or *visitation* with his/her child.

Custodial parents

A *custodial parent* is a parent who is given physical and/or legal custody of a child by court order.

A *child-custody determination* means a judgment, decree, or other order of a court providing for the legal custody, physical custody, or visitation with respect to a child. The term includes a permanent, temporary, initial, and modification order. The term does not include an order relating to child support or other monetary obligation of an individual.[12] Where the child will live with both parents, joint physical custody is ordered, and both parents are custodial parents. Where the child will only live with one of the parents, sole physical custody is ordered, and the parent with which the child lives is the custodial parent, the other parent is the non-custodial parent.

Non-custodial parents

A *non-custodial parent* is a parent who does not have physical and/or legal custody of his/her child by court order.

A *child-custody determination* means a judgment, decree, or other order of a court providing for the legal custody, physical custody, or visitation with respect to a child. The term includes a permanent, temporary, initial, and modification order. The term does not include an order relating to child support or other monetary obligation of an individual.[12] Where the child will only live with one of the parents, sole physical custody is ordered, and the parent with which the child lives is the custodial parent, the other parent is the noncustodial parent. Note, however, where the child will live with both parents, joint physical custody is ordered, and both parent are custodial parents.

Information Provided by Wikipedia
https://en.wikipedia.org/wiki/Child_custody

The Child's Perspective

Mission Statement:

"Helping parents identify disagreements and communicate with understanding from The Child's emotional and psychological view".

As an effort to assist in raising awareness towards the issues that arise throughout co-parenting, Selfish Subjects, Inc. will be conducting events to raise funding for the 5013 non-profit organization The Child's Perspective.

If you would like more information on how you donate to this organization, please log on to www.thechildsperspective.com .

Special Thanks

We'd like to give a special thanks to our readers and supporters, as well as thank each and every parent and child that assisted in bringing this book to fruition. Your testimonial contributions will assist in our mission to bring awareness and understanding of the family matters embedded within these pages.

www.ingramcontent.com/pod-product-compliance
Lightning Source LLC
LaVergne TN
LVHW051056080426
835508LV00019B/1910